THE WORLD ACCORDING TO

Heavy Metal

THE WORLD ACCORDING TO

STEPHEN BLAKE
AND
ANDREW JOHN

MICHAEL O'MARA BOOKS LIMITED

First published in Great Britain in 2002 by
Michael O'Mara Books Limited
9 Lion Yard
Tremadoc Road
London SW4 7NQ

A CIP catalogue record for this book is available from the British
Library

ISBN 1-85479-195-8

1 3 5 7 9 10 8 6 4 2

Designed and typeset by Design 23

Printed and bound in Finland by WS Bookwell, Juva

Contents

With grateful thanks to
Patrick Jeffery
for his help with this book

*'The things that come
to those who wait
may be the things left
by those
that got there first.'*

STEPHEN TYLER of Aerosmith

Introduction:
THE BRILLIANT, THE BARMY
AND THE BIZARRE

'Whatever else I do, my epitaph will be
OZZY OSBOURNE
BORN DECEMBER 3, 1948.
DIED, WHENEVER.
AND HE BIT THE HEAD OFF A BAT.'

Heavy metal inhabits – and is – a world of its own. Look the phrase up in an online encyclopedia or dictionary and your computer will probably pull up things such as lead, copper and curium, and talk of relative densities of 5.0 or higher, rather than produce names such as Iron Maiden, Judas Priest and Megadeth.

As with most musical genres, what is problematical is establishing a starting point. After all, there are those who say The Kinks had heavy-metal elements in their music, while others state that it began with Black Sabbath, and will hear no argument to the contrary.

Yet the reason why you can't simply put heavy metal into a neat box with a date at the beginning and a date at the end is that it *evolved*, and is still evolving. The term 'heavy metal' itself was a part of that evolution. Nobody sat down in a studio or office one day and thought, 'I'll invent heavy metal – loud rock music with an emphasis on beat and long guitar riffs, which will develop into various subgenres such as black metal, doom metal and death metal, and will spawn a number of people who will be heavily into satanic arts and body parts.'

'With this record we
wanted to create music to
bring about the Apocalypse.'

MARILYN MANSON, 1996

Those who think heavy metal is just a load of noise have not heard it beyond the few bars necessary for them to make that dismissive judgement. Within the short phrase 'heavy metal' can be found a spectrum of musical styles that include gruff, guttural vocals and very high, wailing vocals; detuned, slow, sludgy guitar work and highly technical, fast-and-furious guitar work; songs about love; songs about politics; songs about social issues; songs apparently about utter nonsense.

When this often controversial music was growing up during the seventies and eighties, no one could have predicted that the fifty-three-year-old Ozzy Osbourne, former lead singer with Black Sabbath and a self-proclaimed 'nutter', would one day perform at Buckingham Palace at the invitation, no less, of HM (that's 'Her Majesty', not 'heavy metal') the Queen, as he did at her Golden Jubilee pop concert in June 2002. There he was among 'respectable' (many would say boring) acts such as Cliff Richard, as well as still-wet-behind-the-ears newbies like Will Young, 2002 winner of the TV series *Pop Idol*.

'I'm always surprised at how I look.'

MARILYN MANSON, 1996

To many, heavy metal has been characterized by its obsession with matters pathological and satanic, not to mention scatological. Just take a look at some of the names of the bands that come under the heading of 'extreme metal': Pungent Stench, Venom, Pestilence, Dismember, Macabre, Septic Flesh, Vomitory, Malevolent Creation and Grave – and they're just the prettier-sounding ones.

'I can't even say the word [disco]: it's too early in the day to get upset.'

**BON SCOTT of AC/DC
(speaking in the seventies)**

Then there's hair, not just on the top of the head. There was the glam era of heavy metal (and rock, of course), when head hair was *big*, not to mention lacquered, but it's also to be found on the faces of many exponents of metal. Tattoos are also very much in evidence, as are studs, ear- and nose rings and other metal adornments that make you wonder how these guys get from the stage to the tour bus. Add to that often extreme clothing and accoutrements – and sometimes even more extreme statements or behaviour, on and off stage – and the mix becomes extremely potent.

In the end, the only thing that can be said with any certainty is that it all began *somewhere*, but that it is not possible to be definitive about precisely when or how or why. So the first chapter of this book looks at origins, and is followed by an overview of heavy metal itself. Next comes a section on band profiles. In a book of this size, this can't be as comprehensive as books that are devoted to, say, one era, one subgenre or one band, but here is a collection of profiles some of the better- and lesser-known bands, as well as some of the very big names, such as Judas Priest, Iron Maiden and Black Sabbath.

'To be creative you gotta be a child. You gotta be true to the crib.'

STEVEN TYLER of Aerosmith

The next chapter, 'Any Old Iron', is a miscellaneous collection of items from the world of heavy metal – odds and ends that are quirky, extreme, eccentric, enlivening, funny but, at all events, interesting. In that chapter, too, is a look at all those confusing subgenres: doom metal, thrash metal, death metal, black metal, goth metal and several others besides.

Finally, there is a chapter devoted to that self-confessed nutter mentioned above, Ozzy Osbourne, seen by many as the daddy and granddaddy of heavy metal. As this book goes to press, he is approaching his fifty-fourth birthday, and is probably as popular, and even more widely known, than he has ever been since the start of his astonishing career in the late sixties.

Naturally, there is a whole library of books out there devoted to this genre. In contrast, *The World According to Heavy Metal* is a miscellany, a taster, an overview with examples, something to whet readers' appetites and to introduce them to this vibrant, creative, often weird, sometimes bizarre and occasionally creepy world – the world of heavy metal.

ANDREW JOHN AND STEPHEN BLAKE,
August 2002

'I don't need to speak ...
I play the guitar!'

JOE PERRY of Aerosmith

Before the Beginning:
METAL'S MIXED ANCESTRY

*'Whether it's fine artists, musical artists,
or ultra right-wing bullshit artists,
we all need the right to
freedom of expression.'*

STEVEN TYLER of Aerosmith

et's talk about music. For without music there wouldn't have been music, in a manner of speaking. The causal link can go back as long as there has been music – to whenever the caveman first clobbered his woman on the head with a club, then clobbered the woman of the chap next door (you know, the one with the poncy tiger-skin suit and the flat-pack cave furniture) and realized there were two distinct notes. So he got twelve of them lined up and invented the chromatic scale. You get the drift. A begat B begat C . . .

Before heavy metal there was rock. There was rock

and roll. There was blues. There was honky-tonk. You name it, and you can bet your bottom dollar that it will have had its due influence on metal.

There are those who say true rock and roll died in 1959. Quite how they can put such a distinct date on it is anyone's guess – but who are we to argue? What followed, in the sixties, was a pale imitation, some say. Well, it would be: that's probably when we saw the over-commercialization of the genre begin, and it's all been downhill from there. Or has it?

Heavy metal, like its predecessors, began with rebellion: rebellion against previous musical forms; rebellion against the corporatism that would like to have the music business all to its avaricious self; rebellion against the generation above this one and its norms and anally retentive attitudes to sex and lifestyle. Without rebellion, the human race wouldn't move on. It's part of what moves us forward. And so it is with music.

So what were its precursors, and how closely can we see their influences in the forms of metal we hear today: black metal, death metal, extreme metal (largely influenced by Lemmy of Motörhead), thrash metal, doom metal? Metal fans will find the answers to the second part of the question in their chosen forms, no doubt (and argue over their beer till the cows come home), while others will say, 'What? Elvis? In that cacophonous row?'

Let us look briefly at the fifties and sixties, beginning with the singer whose 'Rock Around the Clock' in 1954 put rock and roll on the proverbial map, for it was the first of its kind to gain wide appeal. William John Clifton ('Bill') Haley (1925–81) was a country-and-western bandleader from Pennsylvania. 'Rock Around the Clock' sold more than 25 million copies.

Earlier records, such as 'Rock the Joint' and 'Crazy Man Crazy' had set him on the road to what would become his trademark rock-and-roll style, and for many he was where it began. So popular did Haley become that he had twelve singles in the US Top Forty in 1955–6.

'We steer completely clear
of anything suggestive.
We take a lot of care with
lyrics because we don't want to
offend anybody.
The music is the main thing and
it's just as easy to write
acceptable words.'

BILL HALEY

Bill Haley doesn't conjure up the word 'rebellion' in your mind when you look back from the late-Ozzy era (Osbourne, that is, the man who infamously bit the head off a live bat on stage in Iowa in 1982, and went on to entertain Her Gracious Majesty Queen Elizabeth II at her own palace in the summer of 2002). However, in those days the man with the kiss curl epitomized rebellion and his movies provoked riots in cinemas.

Rock and roll was the first type of rock music, and was – but of course – born in the USA. It came – just as metal and punk would do in the sixties and seventies – as a rebellion. This particular mutiny was that of the emerging postwar youth culture, and was based mainly on the music of the South. Rock and roll owed its existence to the 'jump blues' form of R&B, while barrelhouse, honky-tonk and boogie-woogie are all to be found there if you listen hard enough.

The term 'rock 'n' roll' was introduced by a radio disc jockey called Alan Freed, because he was trying to attract white audiences for what had hitherto been associated with black artists.

The reason why 'true' rock and roll is deemed to have died in 1959 is that the sixties saw session musicians move in, singers collaborate with professional songwriters and composers, pretty boys and girls, individually and in groups (that's what we called them in the sixties, and the terms 'band' and 'group' now seem interchangeable), with adoring fans shrieking in theatres. British bands were playing rock and roll, blues and rhythm and blues in various combinations, and the group (or band) we tend to think of first was The Beatles.

Now *there* was rebellion. Dads would forbid the wearing of Beatle hair or silly Beatle jackets, and Beatle posters were ordered to be removed from bedroom walls. (Well, that was the case with one of our dads, anyway.)

Hard rock, jazz rock and folk rock were also big movements in the sixties, and we were spellbound by such guitar virtuosi as Hendrix and Clapton. Soul music, exemplified by the likes of Aretha Franklin with the gospel influence still intact, came to our pop charts, and names such as James Brown and Marvin Gaye still trip off the tongue when we think of the funky, soulful music of that time.

WITH STRINGS ATTACHED

Since heavy-metal music is guitar-oriented, it may be appropriate to talk now of, well, the guitar – notably the *electric* guitar. The name Stratocaster is inextricably linked with the electric guitar – indeed, this solid-bodied instrument has changed little since the Fender company of the USA introduced it in the mid-fifties, although electric guitars had been in use in America since the thirties, and Leo Fender had brought out the first mass-produced solid-body guitar in the late 1940s.

It was about this time that the American musician and inventor Les Paul developed several prototypes of the electric guitar, and we can pin the start of its popularity to this time. And where would heavy metal be without the efforts of Mr Paul and Mr Fender? Rock music – white rock, anyway – has been dominated by guitars, with the classic line-up being three guitars and a drum kit. Black rhythm and blues used wind instruments more, such as saxes and horns. The keyboard has been common to both brands of music, but the guitar is what drives rock, and drives metal.

The jazz musician Charlie Christian was, in the late 1930s, one of the first to use the electric guitar as a solo instrument, and the first blues man to record using an amplified guitar was T-Bone Walker.

Influences on rock and subsequently on metal came as much from guitar-playing styles as from lyrics and line-ups. Notable among such influences has to be Chuck Berry, who in the fifties brought something unique to guitar playing, and is firmly in the history books as one of rock's all-time greats, rightly acknowledged for the raw energy of his live performances and the complexity of his musical style.

It was Berry, along with Elvis Presley, Little Richard and others who in the 1950s shaped what rock music was to become. Presley brought his own distinctive style to what had already come from the likes of those black artists and surprised many by having a 'black' voice in a white face.

We've already mentioned Jimi Hendrix and Eric Clapton as memorable exponents of the electric guitar. Carlos Santana is another name associated with Hendrix and Clapton, because they all experimented with feedback and distortion, making it a distinct part of the musical experience rather than just an unfortunate mistake. When it *had* been an unfortunate mistake you stuck your fingers in your ears. When it became deliberate, the same sound had fans rapt and gawping with drooling admiration. Funny how things turn out.

The 1960s saw more open-ended musical forms entering the rock repertoire, whereas before the genre had relied mostly on the more traditional structure of the twelve-bar blues and the thirty-two-bar song. Now performers were allowed to be more flexible and versatile. Some artists even borrowed the idea of the suite form from classical music. Thematic structures began to enter the realms of the rock album in the sixties, too, and the 'concept album' was born.

It was also during the sixties that we saw the record producer coming more into prominence, and names such as Phil Spector began to emerge. The record was no longer known by the name of its artist alone, and producers were distinguishable by their 'sound'. Spector's very much wall-to-wall, filling each microsecond of time with noise. Great sound.

One of the most popular styles of the sixties was Motown – so named after the company that produced it, Motown Records. The word comes from 'motor town', because Motown was named after the motor city of Detroit. A fusing of pop and gospel gave Motown its distinctive sound, coupled with appealing melodies. Names like Martha and The Vandellas, Stevie Wonder, Marvin Gaye, The Four Tops, Gladys Knight and The Pips, The Supremes, Smokey Robinson and Mary Wells come to mind as exemplars of the Motown sound, launched as they were by Mr Motown himself, Berry Gordy, who founded the company in 1959.

Other styles that the sixties spawned are the surf sound of the Beach Boys and folk-rock, developed by, among others, Bob Dylan.

The so-called British invasion of the USA was carried out by such bands as The Beatles and The Rolling Stones, causing the inevitable backlash, with artists such as Jimi Hendrix and Creedence

Clearwater Revival rising to the challenge and creating newer, fresher more innovative forms and preventing what had gone before from becoming too formulaic.

However, we mustn't underestimate the effect The Beatles had on rock, notably with the significant, corner-turning 1967 album, *Sgt Pepper's Lonely Hearts Club Band*, which signalled an acceptance of rock as an art form. The Stones, too, made their contribution. They were seen as the bad boys of rock right from the start, creating in the minds of part of the public a negative attitude towards rock music.

As the saying goes, if you remember the sixties, you weren't there. This was the era that brought us psychedelic sounds and mind-altering drugs, notably lysergic acid diethylamide (LSD). We were entering the age of the rock festival. Jerry Garcia and The Grateful Dead jammed away at these happenings while youth culture became more anti-establishment. Against that ethos, though, big names were signing up with big companies for big money, among them the likes of Janis Joplin, Jefferson Airplane and Santana.

Rock hardened noticeably. Volume increased. The guitar was still king, but it was louder, more energetic, sometimes brutal in its ferocity, the wild, raging engine of the music that was to come. One of its exponents we have already mentioned: the great Seattle-born James Marshall ('Jimi') Hendrix, who died at the height of his fame in 1970. With Mitch Mitchell and Noel Redding, Hendrix founded The Jimi Hendrix Experience in England, a band that toured Europe a lot and will be remembered for such hits as 'Hey, Joe' and 'Purple Haze'. Hendrix returned to the States and appeared at the Monterey Festival in 1967, with a memorable performance of 'Wild Thing' (to be seen in the film *Monterey Pop*, released in 1969).

He was a noisy and controversial performer, with his sexy gyrations, his strongly amplified guitar playing and compulsive beat. His guitar playing became something of a blueprint for performers the world over, and his influence on rock and, later, heavy metal is palpable. He famously played 'The Star-Spangled Banner' with his teeth.

Another band well remembered from that festival in Monterey were The Who, notorious for their bad-boy behaviour on stage, where guitars were often smashed against amps.

Meanwhile, in England in 1966, Eric Clapton had come together with Ginger Baker and Jack Bruce to form Cream.

As the sixties came to a close and the seventies began to take over, bands whose names are familiar to all metal fans began to emerge and develop this aggressive and often violent musical form: bands such as Black Sabbath (who were to get the inevitable nickname 'the Sabs'), Led Zeppelin and Deep Purple.

It was dubbed 'slum rock' by the bad boy of metal, Ozzy Osbourne. But it would change its name.

The beginning of the seventies was also the beginning of an era of big change in the rock movement generally, as boundaries between the various forms blurred with the onset of more musical freedom. Those forms included psychedelic rock, hard rock, heavy rock, blues rock, adult-oriented rock and progressive rock.

And the artists who were emerging as significant players bore such names as High Tide, Black Cat Bones, Black Widow, Black Sabbath (of course!), Uriah Heep, Blue Oyster Cult and UFO.

Heavy metal had arrived, and was booked in for a long stay.

Rock Is a Hard Place:
METAL COMES TO STAY

*'I wasn't a goth - I think maybe
I wanted to be but I wasn't cool enough
to fit in. I didn't have the confidence,
I was invisible, totally insignificant.'*

MARILYN MANSON, MAY 1997

The birth of MTV in 1981 allowed everyone to experience the pummelling rhythms and riffs of heavy metal. Before that, ardent fans wrote off for tickets, queued at the doors of venues and bought albums and singles.

Such would have been the case when Black Sabbath burst onto the music scene in a blaze of raucous noise and musical mayhem in 1969. Many see the moment Black Sabbath came into being as the moment heavy metal came into being, although there are many others who would disagree, claiming that the likes of Led Zeppelin were already doing heavy metal by then. One website we consulted says that, according to most metal annals, it began with 'You Really Got Me' by The Kinks (1964) and 'My Generation' by The Who (1965). Those songs seem tame now – but then?

Others say that Alice Cooper really began it all with the formation of his band, The Spiders, way back in 1965. Between 1966 and 1970 several bands came into being, notably Cream, The Jimi Hendrix Experience, Led Zeppelin, Vanilla Fudge, Steppenwolf, Iron Butterfly, Blue Cheer, Deep Purple, Mountain, Grand Funk Railroad, Free, Humble Pie, Uriah Heep, Bloodrock, Cactus, Black Widow and Black Sabbath.

And the first time – as far as we can tell – that the term 'heavy metal' was used was when Steppenwolf, in one of their songs, referred to the sound of a motorbike as 'heavy metal thunder'. It was often referred to as 'classic metal' in the early days because of its pioneering nature.

As well as bands such as The Jimi Hendrix Experience (seen by many metalheads as being in there with Janis Joplin and The Doors as a major rock unit), Cream are cited by commentators as having been in at the start of heavy metal (the band contained the legendary Eric Clapton then, of course). During four years and a number of albums, they influenced the likes of future acts such as Van Halen and Rush.

While bands like Status Quo were hardening their sound somewhat, the outfits that seemed to take over the show were undoubtedly Deep Purple, Black Sabbath and Led Zeppelin. The Satanic imagery of heavy metal enters the stage here, courtesy of Black Sabbath and Led Zeppelin. While the Sabs didn't claim to have any Satanists in their number, many of their lyrics betrayed a fascination with the occult, and the subject also interested Jimmy Page, guitarist with Led Zeppelin. (Page, incidentally, was formerly with The Yardbirds, a band that also contained Clapton and experimented with psychedelic distortion.)

The Satanic theme was to continue, however, with other bands (take just one example: an album by the Norwegian band Immortal called *Diabolical Fullmoon Mysticism*), but Sabbath's Ozzy Osbourne once said that he found it creepy that fans turned up wearing black robes and carrying candles.

*'A lot of times with Lizzy,
things seemed to get so frantic
on stage that sometimes it seemed
more than a little chaotic.'*

SCOTT GORHAM of Thin Lizzy (1980s)

Bands began to do the live shows big time. Stage sets were bigger, on-stage antics more outrageous – especially those of Alice Cooper, which often featured boa constrictors and mutilated female mannequins. For many metalheads, it wasn't until Black Sabbath released their first album, *Black Sabbath*, in 1970 that heavy metal could truly be said to have arrived. The sound said it all: deep, gloomy, crunching chords that would set the scene for later bands such as Anathema, Acrimony and Beseech. Black Sabbath can also claim to have influenced bands like Corrosion of Conformity, Nirvana and Metallica.

Deep Purple, too, were heralded as true innovators, especially after their *Deep Purple in Rock* album, featuring Ian Gillan's shrieks, Ritchie Blackmore's classical training on guitar and Jon Lord's synthesizers.

> *'I put sex in my lyrics because I'm always thinking about it, it's always on my mind.'*

STEVEN TYLER of Aerosmith,
***Globe and Mail*, Toronto, February 1997**

Metal in the mid-seventies saw such bands as Blue Oyster Cult, Thin Lizzy, Judas Priest, Queen, Aerosmith and Kiss rise in popularity, and one of them, Judas Priest, would go down in rock history as popularizers of the idea of *two* guitarists in the line-up.

Queen brought us some majestic melodies, some great harmonies and plenty of innovation; Kiss were great exponents of the live show; and Aerosmith brought back sex, drugs and the blues.

Bands which had hitherto been part of the world of progressive rock were now seen to be taking their music into harder realms – outfits such as Genesis and Pink Floyd, for instance; and Jethro Tull, Yes and King Crimson flirted with heavy metal in songs such as (respectively) 'Aqualung', 'Heart of the Sunrise' and '21st Century Schizoid Man'.

Heavy metal had gone into decline in the mid-seventies with the arrival of punk, with its debt to heavy metal evident in its music, but with the addition of more fury. However, heavy metal proved more resilient than many had perhaps given it credit for, and it coexisted with punk, each genre making its own distinctive mark on the rock-music world.

There were other reasons for this decline, too, with some bands getting into damaging drug habits, others fading after making personnel changes. Led Zeppelin folded in 1980 after its drummer, John Bonham, died of an alcohol overdose. Bands such as Queen and

Judas Priest kept the ball rolling, and others kept going strong, notably Rush and AC/DC.

Another 'big' band was Blackmore's Rainbow, but it, too, faded at the end of the eighties amid internal rows and the departure of Ronnie James Dio.

While punk was still a growing phenomenon among the world's rebellious youth (and those not so youthful), another highly acclaimed band began to impact upon the scene: Motörhead. The terms 'thrash metal', 'speed metal' and 'power metal' come to mind when you think of Motörhead, who would go on to found another subgenre, death metal.

When heavy metal came back into the spotlight it was bands such as Queen, Judas Priest, Accept and the Scorpions who championed it. (It was Judas Priest, incidentally, who popularized the studs, leather and spikes that were to dominate heavy metal for years to come.) Meanwhile, we saw the short-lived but influential NWOBHM – or new wave of British heavy metal, in full. This brought to prominence such performers as Def Leppard, Diamond Head, Iron Maiden, Saxon, Sweet Savage, Samson, Tygers of Pan Tang, Venom and Raven. This was a period that influenced all the subgenres, and all can be traced back in some degree to these pioneers.

Only Def Leppard and Iron Maiden would survive for long, the latter ruling the rock world until the birth of Metallica, who brought thrash metal to the masses after the subgenre had been set in motion by Venom at the beginning of the era of extreme metal. As well as Metallica, Venom went on to inspire such upcoming bands such as Mantas (which would later become Death), Slayer and Exodus.

The USA responded with its own bands, such as Van Halen and the pop/glam-metal explosion in the 1980s. The early part of the decade also saw Mötley Crüe and Ratt, two bands from Los Angeles. Influenced by such bands as Sweet and T-Rex, they wrote accessible material, big on hooks, and glam-influenced, taking images from the likes of Gary Glitter, David Bowie, Alice Cooper, The New York Dolls and Kiss.

Mötley Crüe launched the Los Angeles metal explosion at about that time with *Shout at the Devil*, which brought heavy metal back into the commercial zone, helping other bands to stardom, including the older Twisted Sister, Ratt and Quite Riot. All of this ultimately paved the way for one of the most famous and successful metal bands ever, Bon Jovi.

Both Bon Jovi and Def Leppard took the harshness of metal and blended it with the accessibility of pop, making it just right for MTV audiences. This pop-metal explosion tended to obscure other upcoming bands such as Junkyard, Thunder and G.U.N.

There seemed to be a gap. A newer, harder edge was needed. In came Guns N' Roses. However, accessible bands were not eclipsed by Guns N' Roses, successful though they were, and bands such as Warrant and Poison surfaced, with original and catchy songs and plenty of glam.

Heavy metal might be seen by those who are merely on the fringes – or not particularly interested at all – as an all-male affair, and an all-very-macho-heterosexual-male affair at that. However, as you'll see elsewhere in this book, gays feature in heavy metal, as do women.

It was the pop-metal scene that brought the latter into prominence, with the Runaways and New Wave of British Heavy Metal Girlschool coming to the fore. Joan Jett & The Blackhearts, Lita Ford, Vixen, L7, Phantom Blue and the gloomy Drain S.T.H. were among the female bands to emerge.

*'I think most people know that
I've been a gay man all my life.
It's something I've been comfortable
with for ever.'*

**ROB HALFORD on the
MTV programme** *Superrock*,
February 1998

During the eighties Black Sabbath were still very much about, having become a legend. By now, Ozzy Osbourne had left (in 1978) and the singer was Ronnie James Dio. Two albums, *Heaven and Hell* and *Mob Rules*, marked a change in direction for the Sabs, while a solo Ozzy was releasing, among other things, *Blizzard of Ozz* and *Diary of a Madman*. (See 'The Wizardry of Ozz' for a more detailed look at the life of the daddy of metal.)

A number of seventies bands made comebacks in the eighties, but somehow there would never be that same energy that characterized the early impact they and their music made on the rock scene.

One band that took the scene by storm in the eighties was the spearhead of thrash/speed/power metal, Metallica, formed by Lars Ulrich in 1981 with James Hetfield. With their snarling vocals, multiple riffing and double-pedal drums, Metallica were shunned by MTV and other commercial stations.

Other thrash outfits came onto the scene about this time: Slayer, Anthrax, Megadeth (founded by a former Metallica guitarist, Dave Mustaine). This band pioneered what would later be called techno-thrash: lots of riffs and *very* noticeable tempo changes.

Metallica released *Master of Puppets* in 1986, and this thrust speed metal into the limelight, taking with it, besides Megadeth, bands such as Slayer and Anthrax, and power metal was finding its way in commercial circles.

This was seen by many hard metalheads as the antidote to pop metal, but there were a number of very good bands that didn't achieve the recognition they deserved, among them Metal Church, Coroner, Flotsam and Jetsam, Wrathchild America, Sacred Reich and Anvil during their early days.

Death metal came through thrash metal. This was characterized by bands such as Hellhammer (Jan Axel von Blomberg) with *Apocalyptic Raids*, Death with *Scream Bloody Gore*, Possessed with *The Seven Churches* and Bathory. Not the type of music aimed at commercial success, with guitars that became heavier by the day and tempo changes that went from tortoise to fast to Mach II.

Vocalists' screams turned into almost unintelligible guttural noises, while double-pedalling was *de rigueur* for drummers.

When death metal began to succumb, as all genres do, it was revived by such outfits as Morbid Angel, Sepultura and Obituary. And look at some of the names of other bands that were around at that time: Carcass, Dismember, Benediction, Malevolent Creation, Hypocrisy, Entombed, Edge of Sanity, Deicide and Pestilence – to name but a few.

The later eighties saw grindcore, a subgenre that emanated from death metal but eventually found its own niche and developed its own distinct identity.

Among its best-known exponents were Napalm Death, who dished up their brand of heavy metal with such albums as *Scum*, *Harmony Corrupted* and *Utopia Banished*.

Grindcore is the most radical of heavy metal because of its tendency to 'deconstruct' music. Napalm Death, for instance, forsook harmony and melody in those three albums.

Black metal is a branch of death metal – black being not racial in this context but Satanic. This was death metal made more melodic. Bands that spring to mind are Samael, Satyricon, Cradle of Filth and Moonspell. These bands and others like them incorporated a number of new elements into their music, including classical, folkloric European, flamenco, female singers and synthesizers.

The early nineties saw progressive, doom and classic metal taking over from death, and bands in the spotlight were, among others, Tiamat, Therion, Sentenced, and Cemetary.

Playing as fast as fingers allowed – faster in some cases – became a bit passé for some bands, and they decided to slow things up a little. Enter a revived doom metal, thought to have died out when Ozzy Osbourne left Black Sabbath. It's accepted by many commentators that bands such as Saint Vitus, Trouble and Witchfinder General were among the best exponents of this slower variety of heavy metal.

Doom had mixed fortunes until two bands in particular hit the scene: Paradise Lost and Cathedral. *Gothic*, Paradise Lost's album, even incorporated orchestration and guitar licks and took on a haunting tone. Cathedral were more akin to Black Sabbath.

With the bands that followed these two, doom metal took on a number of new influences, among them operatic vocals and orchestral passages, as well as women's voices.

Out of doom metal came Samhain, formed by Glenn Danzig, who later formed Danzig. Samhain owed some influence to the style of the punk band The Misfits, but it was much heavier. Glenn Danzig disbanded Samhain after the release of *November Coming Fire*, and formed Danzig, who released an eponymous debut album.

Several albums later, and following the 'industrial' metal era of the nineties, Danzig changed direction from their earlier musical style, not dissimilar to Black Sabbath, complete with Satanic imagery. A more traditional metal ensued from Danzig, along with such outfits as Loudness and the former Mercyful Fate member, King Diamond. Diamond moved away from speed metal and incorporated grunts and high-pitched wailing into his style.

So diverse has heavy metal become, and, indeed, was becoming in the late eighties and throughout the nineties, that even the trademark high vocals were dropped by some bands, in favour of instruments only. Prime among them were Joe Satriani, Steve Vai and Yngwie Malmsteen. Satriani was a guitar virtuoso, and Vai was his student.

Malmsteen is said to have a big ego, but on the plus side he was being hailed for his dexterity and classical-music influence.

Alternative metal began to die out in the mid-nineties. Nirvana were no more after the death of Kurt Cobain. Pearl Jam were no longer touring because of a legal problem with Ticketmaster and the singer Layne Staley's drug habit meant that Alice in Chains were no longer touring as much. Bands began – as they had in the eighties – to repeat tried and trusted formulas – although two that stood out were Smashing Pumpkins and Helmet.

> *'The first person we played our demo to said it was "beat-up-your-Mom music".'*
>
> **MARILYN MANSON, April 1998**

Another revival of heavy metal began in the latter half of the nineties. This can be put down to the harder-edged sound that emerged as well as the influence of comeback and reunion tours and appearances by the likes of Kiss, The Sex Pistols, Jimmy Page and Robert Plant, Slaughter, Quiet Riot, Ratt, Black Sabbath, Mötley Crüe, Warrant and Poison.

A nineties metal phenomenon was known as rap metal, or rap-core. Groups such as Anthrax, Bad Brains and Aerosmith had already been experimenting with it. It was pioneered largely by Body Count and Rage Against the Machine.

Marilyn Manson came along and shocked the world almost overnight with screams and his show of pure evil. The album *Antichrist Superstar* offended some liberals as well as conservatives. *Time* magazine once put Marilyn Manson in the same league as Kiss.

As the nineties wore to a close, power groove and industrial were two dominant forces in the heavy-metal scene, and Trent Reznor was seen by some commentators to have taken over where Kurt Cobain left off. Machine Head, Fear Factory, Atari Teenage Riot and Strapping Young Lad are some of the names that spring to the minds of metalheads.

And, of course, Ozzy Osbourne is still up there wowing audiences. Aged fifty-three at the time of writing (he will be fifty-four in December 2002), he was heading the heavy-metal extravaganzas known as Ozzfest, which have featured such names as a reunited Black Sabbath, Fear Factory, Pantera and Sepultura.

Line-ups have changed over the years, but typically a heavy-metal outfit will consist of the usual bass, rhythm and lead guitars, plus a drummer, often playing two bass drums (Lars Ulrich of Metallica, for instance). The guitar is what drives heavy metal, with heavy and sometimes melodic riffs and some intricate solos.

Vocals, too, have varied, be it high-pitched wailing of deep guttural, growling. Often the lyrics can't be heard at all, but this doesn't seem to worry performers or fans. Pity, really, because some of the lyrics are worth listening to!

Among the best-known names in the world of heavy metal – and you'll find some of them featured in this book – are Anthrax, Black Sabbath, Blue Oyster Cult, Burzum, Deep Purple, Deicide, Danzig, Darkthrone, Led Zeppelin, Limp Bizkit, Linkin Park, Yngwie J Malmsteen, Marilyn Manson, Megadeth, Metallica, Mötley Crüe , Motörhead, Obituary, Saxon, Tool and WASP.

To end this chapter, here are brief descriptions of those subgenres we mentioned earlier, though, obviously, mere words can't do full justice to the music, lyrics and performance.

POWER METAL

This is an exception to the rule of unintelligible vocals. Vocals in power metal are usually clean, and there are almost hymnlike choruses.

The lyrics mostly sum up the themes of fantasy or science fiction.

Among the exponents of this brand are Helloween, Hammerfall and Blind Guardian, and many bands have looked to Iron Maiden for their inspiration.

THRASH METAL

Overkill, Slayer, Megadeth, Anthrax and Metallica come to mind as exponents of this brand of metal, with its sixteenth-note strumming. Although it's seen as a bit passé now, it was a giant in its eighties heyday.

It's sometimes referred to as speed metal, although there are those who argue that speed is more technical and cleaner-sounding. Basically, it's rhythm-based and very aggressive.

DEATH METAL

This is characterized by low-pitched guitars and growling, often vomited, vocals, and is often performed at the tempo of speed metal. It's a more brutal sound.

There are two distinct schools of death metal: that of the eighties and that of the mid- to late nineties, which is more melodious and has a cleaner vocal style. Themes include war (Bold Thrower, for instance), Christian (Mortification) and splatter (Cannibal Corpse).

GOTH METAL

Here we find the aggressive styles of heavy metal fused with the icy atmosphere of goth rock. There's an obsession with the theatrical here, too, and religious and horror themes are to be found in the lyrics.

Some exponents of this subgenre have been My Dying Bride, Theatre of Tragedy and Paradise Lost.

GRINDCORE

Much metal isn't known for long songs. This takes punk-length songs and is an extension of death metal, with a lot of misanthropic subjects.

Gore metal

This is gross. It's a form of death or grindcore, but takes the subject matter for its lyrics from pathology manuals and medical texts.

Black metal

This, too, can be conveniently split into an eighties version and a nineties version. The highly theatrical outfits Bathory of Sweden and Mercyful Fate of Denmark were among the leading exponents of this brand, characterized by its Satanic lyrics. The stage shows were quite hammy, and Mercyful Fate's King Diamond was the first major performer to use corpse paint, as it's known: black and white makeup to make the face look skull-like.

The nineties saw a new wave of bands mainly in Sweden and Norway. They used 'blastbeats' – very fast drumming on snare and bass drums – and some frenetic riffing on guitars with vocals that were either screamed or sneered. Exponents of this subgenre were Burzum, Immortal, Darkthrone and Mayhem.

DOOM METAL

Mood and feel and a paranoid darkness characterize this form of metal, reminiscent of the Black Sabbath guitarist Tony Iommi. Tempos are slow and the vocals are deep and menacing.

Gothic influences came into play with bands such as Sisters of Mercy, and in the nineties a variation on a theme was introduced in the form of doomdeath, which mixed death metal with the misery of doom.

NEOCLASSICAL METAL

All the elements of heavy metal are here, plus the fact that the music is all based on baroque styles and structures. Paganini, Bach and Vivaldi can all be heard here and there, and its best-known exponent is perhaps the Swede Yngwie Malmsteen.

Classical elements in both metal and rock are to be found with Ritchie Blackmore of Deep Purple and Eddie Van Halen.

Any Old Iron:
A METAL MISCELLANY

*'It all came from being young,
frustrated, hard-working punk rockers
and not having any food or beers
or any money or anyone trying to
get into your pants.'*

**ROBBIN CROSBY of Ratt, on how
his band made the big time**

The world of metal, like the world of anything, has its mythology. Not every story can be included, but we've picked out a few odds and sods . . .

Like how can you be gay and a metalhead? Well, you can, and there's no reason why not. But it fazes some people, apparently, because they devote whole website features to the subject . . .

And how about the Osbourne daughter who put the kettle on and nearly set the kitchen alight, not realizing that she'd put an electric kettle on the stove? And all that went out on British and American TV . . .

What do a cobra and the Metallica founder and drummer Lars Ulrich have in common? Well, spell it 'CoBrA', and you may realize it's got nothing to do with snakes. It's art, in fact . . .

And how could we not mention Skipknot, the outrageously disgusting Iowa heavy-metal outfit who have a nice line in projectile vomiting? It's all here.

But we begin with the eighties phenomenon Ratt. Did you know they chose that name because a giant US corporation didn't like what they were originally called?

WHEN MICKEY MOUSE RATTED ON MICKEY RAT

There was a lot of hair about in the world of heavy metal in the eighties. It was very camp, in a theatrical sort of way. Mötley Crüe, Cinderella and Poison were noted for the coiffured look, as were Ratt. It was known as hair metal.

The driving force behind Ratt was Robbin Crosby, who died in Los Angeles on 6 June 2002, having been diagnosed HIV-positive eight years earlier. Crosby, noted for his tousled blond hair, co-wrote Ratt's biggest hit, 'Round and Round'. Ratt sold more than 10 million albums in the US alone, and Crosby earned himself the nickname 'The King'.

But that name? Well, guitarist Crosby always wanted to be a musician, and, after he graduated from high school, he played in a band called Phenomenon. Then he formed a band called Mickey Rat, with Stephen Piercy on vocals and Warren DeMartini on guitar. However, typical of huge corporations – especially American ones – the Disney organization objected to the name, and so Mickey Rat became Ratt.

The band had to work hard for their fame, but their dogged determination won the day for them, causing Crosby to remark, 'It all came from being young, frustrated, hard-working punk rockers and not having any food or beers or any money or anyone trying to get into your pants. At that time, what was going on in rock 'n' roll was basically studs and leather. Along with Mötley Crüe, we added a certain glam element.'

Ratt issued their debut album in 1983, and supported Ozzy Osbourne on tour the following year. Their huge single 'Round and Round' led to a video featuring the comedian Milton Berle, and it ensured that Ratt sold more than 4 million copies of their album.

But it wasn't only in the States that Ratt proved

popular. They played Donington in the eighties and three of their albums, *Invasion of Your Privacy* (1985), *Dancing Undercover* (1986) and *Reach for the Sky* (1988) managed to get into the UK album charts but did far better Stateside.

Ratt disbanded in the early nineties with the advent of grunge and Nirvana, but DeMartini and the drummer Bobby Blotzer re-formed the band with a different line-up, and Crosby brought out solo albums.

He spent his last few years in and out of hospital, and told the world he had AIDS during an interview on the Los Angeles radio station KNAC. Blotzer said of Crosby, 'Robbin was put through hell and never, ever bitched about it. That's what made him the king of the world!'

WHAT A DIFFERENCE A GAY MAKES!

Heavy-metal music a gay phenomenon? Don't be ridiculous!

When its performers, exponents and fans have more piercings than St Sebastian, carry more metal about them than a Cunard liner and strut their stuff like Mike Tyson in torn jeans on a bad day, you just don't think of sensitivity to curtain colours and a culinary genius for quiche.

Actually, there's no reason why you shouldn't. But these are the convenient pigeonholes that both gay men and heavy metal have been slotted into, and many people somehow just don't think of the two at the same time and with the same cluster of brain cells.

After all, heavy metal is about heavy machismo, and oozes masculinity and heterosexuality – not that those two always go together.

Yet attempts have been made to suggest that heavy metal – certainly the eighties varieties – was full of gay symbolism, even if not all the artists were queer. And so it's worth a light diversion to study what some aficionados say.

One website we visited looked at the names of albums – names such as *Muscle of Love* by Alice Cooper, *Rock in a Hard Place* by Aerosmith and *Love is for Suckers* by Twisted Sister (not to mention *Open Up and Say . . . Aaah! Native Tongue* by Poison).

Well, you could make the point that these apply equally to heterosexuals.

Then there are the names of some of the bands: Lizzy Borden, Alice Cooper, Thin Lizzy, Cinderella. But does calling yourself 'The Beatles' suggest a bunch of insects who can't spell, or does taking the sobriquet 'The Rolling Stones' mean you never accumulate any moss?

What about the way some of the bands and artists look? Long, teased hair, for instance, well sprayed with lacquer? Then there are tight leather pants – usually black – and black leather vests without shirts. Thigh-high boots and studded belts make up the gay imagery for some observers, while make-up is another.

One wag points out that the heavy-metal guys overcompensate by shagging groupies and dating beautiful women, ensuring they're seen in public as often as possible. While they're doing this, their stage antics point to the mincing queen: wriggling around and the head-banging motion that suggests oral sex with a man.

'Down there [in Texas] they've got the richest groupies in the world. Some of the groupies followed our jet in their private jet.'

JIMMY PAGE of Led Zeppelin

One heavy-metal website we visited lists all of these things and a few more besides and concludes that it has 'incontrovertible evidence' that heavy-metal music is gay, adding, 'Not that there's anything wrong with that.'

One icon of the metal scene we know to be gay is Judas Priest's Rob Halford. Born in Walsall, England, in 1951, he was a member of Judas Priest (formed in the 1960s) after a spell as a theatrical lighting engineer.

He left Priest along with its drummer Scott Travis after he'd formed another band, Fight, which would perform the kind of music he thought wasn't really appropriate for Priest.

Fight did tours, and one album, *A Small Deadly Space*, touched on AIDS issues. He formed a new band, Halford, in 1996.

In April 1998, *Gay Times* carried a piece on Halford:

> *Rob Halford, former lead singer of demonic metal band Judas Priest, has come out as gay. No surprise there then, you might think. Everyone suspected as much years ago as he strutted his stuff in leathers and Muir cap on the cusp between the camp end of heavy metal and hard end of Queen.*

He was there again in the very next issue, under the byline of Richard Smith:

> *Rob Halford was one of those in-but-out stars who walked it like he didn't talk it. Even though he wasn't prepared to declare his sexuality in interviews, he found a way of announcing it in certain lyrics and through his dress codes – something that straight*

*people have got far better at reading recently.
Immediately prior to his coming out, Q magazine
was calling his Eighties model 'a gurning, shrieking,
leather-clad, stud-encrusted pantomime dame whose
stage wardrobe included a leather cap, handcuffs and
bullwhip'. Rob Halford was Heavy Metal's one-man
Village People.*

*Much of the chatter about Rob Halford, both
before and after his coming out, centred on the sheer
incongruity of it all: 'A gay heavy metal star –
whatever next?'*

(Rob Halford, incidentally, temporarily fronted the
band Black Sabbath in November 1992 when their
lead singer Ronnie James Dio refused to take the stage
at the Pacific Amphitheater in Los Angeles.)

Another website surmises that the song 'Locked
and Loaded' is about blow jobs, and quotes part of the
lyric: 'I'll bring you to your knees/And give you what
you please . . ./I'm gonna shoot it . . .'

One web author talks of the hairdos of the outfits
and cites Poison, Ratt and Mötley Crüe and remarks
that their 'lead singers looked like worn-out, third-
rate drag queens'.

There was also Freddie Mercury, of course. He
managed to combine his Queenly antics with some
pretty heavy music both during Queen's heavy-metal
years and their more pop-oriented days. He made it a

fine art, with his clone moustache and T-shirt, his muscularity and writhing stage antics.

Iron Maiden are known for their skip-across-the-stage antics, and commentators have noted the homoeroticism when a band member will hold his guitar for the singer Bruce Dickinson to play.

Statistics are not available to show how many gays there are in the heavy-metal scene, because finding statistics on *anything* sexual that involves telling the truth about oneself is damn-near impossible. So we can bet that, statistically speaking (even though those stats don't exist), there are as many gay guys in the metal scene in proportion to the heterosexuals as there are in any part of the entertainment industry – and it's an industry where gay genius is abundant, whether it's in music, acting or writing.

While we're not going to see a sudden rush of gay-boy metal bands, it's worth taking a look at a lyric from Halford's 'Resurrection': 'I rid the demons from my heart/And found the truth was with me from the start.'

And we know there are others out there, if what Rob Halford told *USA Today* is true: 'I think it's just great to acknowledge that there are many gay heavy-metal fans in the world, and I'm proud to know that they support and love the music as much as my other fans do.'

LARS BANGS THE DRUM FOR ART

While the frenetic drummer with Metallica, Lars Ulrich, is not flailing his arms around creating a wall of percussion sound in a frenzied display on stage, he's probably gazing thoughtfully at a painting.

In May 2002 he sold some of his art collection and raised £9.1 million in order to build a house on a 200-acre mountain site near San Francisco. Five paintings were sold at the Rockefeller Center, including a 1982 work by Jean-Michel Basquiat called *Profit I*, which went for £3.7 million. This was a record for the artist. He sold further paintings in London the following month.

Ulrich became fascinated by a group of painters from Copenhagen, Brussels and Amsterdam, collectively known as the CoBrA artists. He maintains that looking at art helped him to cope with the stresses of the music industry. Indeed, he began visiting art galleries in cities where Metallica played.

KNOT OF THIS WORLD

When Slipknot were at a signing in Glasgow in February 2002, one teenage male maggot (the band call their fans maggots) was beside himself with joy. Referring to Slipknot's singer Corey Taylor, he told a reporter, 'I met Corey. He was fantastic! I asked him if he would spit on me – and he did!'

'People are a fucking disaster all across the world. Slipknot preach individualism, and we help our maggots [fans] to get rid of conformity. We're not formula, and nobody is going to break us. Slipknot are going to achieve more in two or three albums than most bands manage in their entire careers.'

SHAWN CRAHAN of Slipknot, *Guardian*, February 2002

A twelve-year-old girl with kohl-stained tears running down her face owed her emotional state to having just met members of the overall-clad band at this Glasgow signing. 'I'm so happy that I could puke,' she told the same reporter from the *Guardian*.

Slipknot whip up that sort of behaviour in their maggots. Projectile-vomiting is one of the specialities of band members, certainly the one who has shaped this Iowa-formed outfit since it set up in the mid-nineties, Clown (a.k.a. Shawn Crahan). He is known to take on stage a jar containing the carcass – the rather *old* carcass – of a crow, decomposing *quite* nicely. He opens the jar, takes a sniff and heaves up the junk food he's been eating before the gig.

Another band member, Chris Fehn, goes under the name Dicknose, because of the proboscis that sticks out of the mask he wears. He masturbates this on stage – while, allegedly, the bass player, Paul Gray, occasionally masturbates for real inside his overalls between songs.

Other band members have their own ways of delighting their maggots, often pissing and defecating on stage and, as Corey told the *Guardian*, 'tossing turds' around, adding, 'Dude, our show is completely brutal.'

Few would disagree with that.

Encouraged by Clown's crow-sniffing antics, one fan took him a present (not strictly the done thing among the maggots, but this kid decided to step out of line). What was the gift that hit the mark so well with the kid's hero? 'That dude gave me a four-week-old dead rabbit foetus, man,' he told the *Guardian* reporter. 'I'm flattered. It's not gross to me, and if it's gross to you then fuck you!'

Not the sort of thing you'd say to the thousand-strong Knitting and Crochet Guild, but with a name like Slipknot you're bound to cause confusion, as happened when maggots got to the genteel guild's website by mistake. They'd stumbled across it, as is so easy to do with powerful search engines, by inputting the word 'slipknot'. The guild, you see, has a magazine of that name.

'We've used the name *Slipknot* since 1978,' Rita Taylor of the guild told BBC Online. 'If there's a problem then the band can change its name. But, if they want us to teach them how to knit themselves new masks, we'd be happy to help.'

The purpose of the *Guardian* piece was to report a Valentine's Day signing at a Virgin Megastore, at which maggots' T-shirts bore the legend (inspired by a Slipknot album, of course), 'Fuck it all. Fuck this world. Fuck everything that you stand for. Don't belong, don't exist, don't give a shit! Don't ever judge me!'

EN FAMILLE AVEC OZZY

Our chapter on the great daddy of metal Ozzy Osbourne will tell you he's no ordinary geezer. In fact, he's an absolute nutter of the first order. But one of MTV's most popular shows – which began airing on British television in May 2002 – is a fly-on-the-wall documentary about the Osbourne family at their Beverly Hills home.

And one reviewer – Robin Hanks, writing in the *Independent* – thought Ozzy's family life was 'suffocatingly normal'.

There's a nice nuclear family with just over 2.4 children – three, in fact. OK, Jack, who was sixteen at the time of the programme, likes to wander around the house and grounds in combat gear, and his sister Kelly, who wears pink hair, has been known to set the kitchen on fire. In the first episode, she put the *electric* kettle (you know, the thing with a flex and a plug) on the stove to boil water. Oh, and the kids fight a bit and there's some rather interesting language.

> *'My kids mean more to me than anything else in this poxy world.'*
>
> ## OZZY OSBOURNE

But what comes over from this series is just how much affection – almost palpable – emanates from the stage demon Ozzy for his wife and his kids.

NETTING IT

Since Metallica challenged Napster, forcing it to close and then reappear in a rather diluted form, music and the Internet have always been closely linked.

You can listen to new stuff via your phone line, and, with ADSL and ISDN becoming more widely available, music can be downloaded all the more quickly.

In the traditional world of getting music from artist to listener – via a record company – there would be the A&R people, who would decide which were the good bands and which were the bad (or which were the bands likely to increase the profits of the record company and which were those that wouldn't).

The beauty of the Internet is that you can find all sorts of music put there by beginners who haven't managed a record deal – and they can be anywhere in the world. Of course, you'll need to be able to burn (write to) a CD if you don't want your newly downloaded gems permanently stuck on your hard drive – but many computers come with CD writers on board.

The advantage for the budding musicians is that they can upload their stuff and know that it is being avidly searched for by metalheads (and other music lovers, of course) the world over. The more bands who do this, though, the less dosh there is to go around, and so the chances of making megabucks is going down. But you never know: your band could be one of the lucky ones who get a good, healthy fan base. Most download sites have a way of charging money for the music, so it's a case of getting together enough of it to produce your own CD. After all, if you've got this far, it means you have enough fans to buy it once it's been produced and packaged.

There are cheats, of course – those who brazenly

upload music to free sites. But, in the world of music, 'twas ever thus. Bootlegged records have been around since records themselves have been around. Let's just hope, for the sake of getting new music to a panting audience, that there are enough people willing to play the game, pay up, enjoy the music and go back for more.

AFTER 11 SEPTEMBER

In contrast to some of the behaviour or comments described in this chapter, a number of heavy-metal bands put messages on their websites after the terrorist attacks on the World Trade Center and the Pentagon on 11 September 2001.

Puya

I want to express my deepest sympathy to anyone that in any way was affected by this monstrosity. I think that who ever was capable of pulling this one off is an example of the lowest form of human existence. Such a person does not deserve to be in this world among the rest of us. I do not encourage war by any means, but I think these people need to be found and hung by the balls until they bleed to the most painful death imaginable. It is amazing how humans can be the most intelligent of all the species in this planet, and with the most compassion and admiration towards all living things, and at the same time we are the most self-destructive and vicious of them all . . .

Anthrax
Our hearts go out to everyone . . . the skyline will never be the same again.

Pantera
There are no words worthy to express the sorrow we feel for those who lost loved ones in yesterday's terrible tragedy.

Manowar
The members of Manowar and the staff of the Kingdom of Steel thank you for your e-mail and thoughts following the tragic events of Tuesday, September 11, 2001. Our friends and family in the New York City, Pennsylvania, and Washington, DC, areas are safe and accounted for; however, our thoughts and prayers go out to the families affected by this tragedy. We also hail and salute the police officers, firemen, doctors, volunteers and other workers who have been a part of the rescue effort.

Moonspell

I hope our music can be of any comfort to people affected who know us. We wish the responsible cowards will be found and punished and that the world can learn its own path, finally, into some better harmony than the one we have now. Let us reflect and learn and dream about a better mankind and world, free of fanaticism and ignorance. That is our only wish. Hope we all survive these times of darkness.

Twisted Sister

The extraordinary enormity of the terrorist attacks has affected us all very deeply. We are proud Americans and prouder New Yorkers. We come from Manhattan, Staten Island, the Bronx, Nassau and Suffolk counties. Our lives are all intertwined with the fabric of relationships many of which, through varying degrees of separation, have been affected by this tragedy. We mourn for the workers in WTC. We mourn for the heroic firemen and policemen who gave their lives so unselfishly to save their fellow man. We pray for all of the victims and their families.

Metal Lives:
POTTED BIOGS FROM
THE WORLD OF METAL

'I don't need to speak . . . I play the guitar!'

JOE PERRY of Aerosmith

Yes, metal certainly lives, and will continue to do so, in one form or another – or many. But for this chapter title we had in mind the noun, the one that rhymes with 'knives'.

This isn't an exhaustive chapter of biographies of bands and artists. There are whole books devoted to band biogs, and, indeed, to single biogs of just one band or artist. But we've chosen some of the more interesting and in some cases lesser-known ones, with quite a few taken from that growing phenomenon, extreme metal. After all, this is an overview – the metal aficionados among you will, doubtless, have doctorates in the subject.

Here there is a concentration on some of the bigger

names, and includes some disputed ones, such as Led Zeppelin. Did they remain within the blues/rock tradition, or did they step into – and, indeed, become part of the birth of – heavy metal? Decide for yourself.

This chapter, then, is a snapshot of the bands, listing some of their noted albums and the type of music they were or are into. Some may even have disappeared off the face of the earth by the time you read this.

The names are interesting, too – those that evoke doom, destruction, gloom and all that's gothic. There's no bias on our part in putting the bands that begin with 'A' first and those that begin with 'Z' last. That's just the way the alphabet goes.

AC/DC

Two Glasgow-born brothers, Angus and Malcolm Young, formed this band, which is inextricably associated with the early days of heavy metal, in Sydney in 1973. Phillip Rudd, Bon Scott and Mark Evans made up the rest of the band, and rock bands such as the Rolling Stones are among the influences on their theatrical brand of heavy metal.

They moved to Britain in 1976, and their stage shows were something to be seen, memorable for their theatricality as well as the trademark school uniform worn by Angus Young.

Let There Be Rock came out in 1977, followed by *Powerage* in 1978. If there's one single that is associated with AC/DC it must be 'Rock 'n' Roll Damnation', which preceded *Highway to Hell*, the million-selling album that was released in 1979.

Just like John Bonham of Led Zeppelin, Bon Scott died of an alcohol overdose in February 1980, and his place in the line-up was taken by a former member of the band Geordie, Brian Johnson.

AC/DC quickly became a band who filled stadiums, and their album *Back in Black* topped the UK charts in 1980, while getting them known in the United States.

Their single 'Big Gun' was used in the Arnold Schwarzenegger movie *Last Action Hero* and made it into the UK charts. They recorded the album *Ballbreaker* in 1995.

ACID

Acid were formed in Belgium in 1980, a simple thrash band with Kate de Lombaerd on vocals, T-Bone and Anvill on bass and drums, and Demon and Dizzy Lizzy on guitar.

Acid were largely influenced by Venom. There were some tours but they split up after three albums: *Acid* (1983), *Manic* (1983) and *Engine Beast* (1985).

ACRIMONY

This outfit are from Swansea in Wales, and it was on the strength of a demo disc that they signed up to the Belgian label, Shiver. They formed up in 1991 (with Dorian Walters on vocals, Lee Davies and Stuart O'Hara on guitars, Paul Bidmead on bass and Darren Ivey on drums) and went in for psychedelia and doom, so here was a retro rock reminiscent of the 1970s and some early Black Sabbath.

They split up in 1999 having produced an EP and a couple of good albums, *Hymns to the Stone* (1995) and *Tumuli Shroomaroom* (1997).

AEROSMITH

Aerosmith were formed in 1970 by Steven Tyler (real name, Steven Victor Tallarico) and Joe Perry (both now in their fifties). Tyler – who is the father of actress Liv Tyler (*Stealing Beauty*, *Lord of the Rings* etc.) – had already released a single, and Perry invited him to play in his own band, Chain Reaction.

> *'If we hang ourselves, it's going to be on the tree of creativity.'*
>
> STEVEN TYLER of Aerosmith

They took on other members to complete their line-up, and after playing their first gig they hit on the name Aerosmith, and went on to become one of America's most popular hard-rock outfits. Their first album, *Aerosmith*, was issued in 1973 after the band had been seen gigging by Clive Davies of Columbia Records. This was followed by *Get Your Wings*, released in 1974, and *Toys in the Attic* (1975), which has sold more than 6 million copies worldwide. Within months of being released, their fourth album, *Rocks* (1976) managed platinum status.

'Slash looks like Joe, Joe looks like Keith,
I look like Mick, Mick looks like a black man,
black man invented the blues,
blues had a baby and names
it rock 'n' roll, and Dude
looks like a lady an' all that other stuff.'

STEVEN TYLER of Aerosmith

Some critics were not so keen on the band during this period. They were accused of being derivatives of Led Zeppelin, and, because Tyler bore a physical resemblance to Mick Jagger, comparisons were drawn with the Rolling Stones.

'They are very young, these people
that buy records in America.
They may be intelligent,
but they are unsophisticated.'

MICK JAGGER, 1982

They had the dubious distinction of appearing as a band called Future Villain in the movie *Sgt Pepper's Lonely Hearts Club Band*.

Despite the band's success, Tyler and Perry fell out, and Perry left the band after the album *Night in the Ruts* (1979) and founded the Joe Perry Project. Another band member, Brad Whitford, left in 1981, but, during a 1984 tour, contact was made with Tyler and Whitford, everyone kissed and made up, and the endearing fivesome line-up became an item again.

'A lot of times you see people in the audience
with little kids. If I see that in the audience
I'll tell one of the security guards
to give them earplugs.'

TOM HAMILTON of Aerosmith

More albums followed, including *Done With Mirrors* in 1985, *Permanent Vacation* in 1987, right through to this century, whose first Aerosmith album was *Just Push Play* in 2001. In the meantime, albums had included *Pump* (1989), *Get a Grip* (1993), *Nine Lives* (1997) and *A Little South of Sanity* (1998).

'I can tell you one thing… I would cut this interview off right now if Janis Joplin were playing across the street.'

STEVEN TYLER of Aerosmith, in a 1994 interview

Aerosmith are one of the few bands who can claim a career that spans four decades.

AFFLICTED

Jesper Thorsson (guitar), Michael van de Graff (vocals), Yasin Hillborg (drums) and Christian Canalez (bass) produced two black-metal albums in the early and mid-1990s, but split in 1995 after a less than enthusiastic welcome for their second album, *Dawn of Glory* (1995).

Their first album had been *Prodigal Sun* in 1992. After they split, they began a new band called Molosser.

AGGRESSOR

This lot formed as a death-metal band with Alex Colin-Tocquaine on guitar and vocals, Manu Ragot on guitar, Joel Guigou on bass and Steiphan Gwegwam on drums.

They produced four albums before they split in 1995: *Satan's Sodomy* (1987), *Neverending Destiny* (1990), *Towards Beyond* (1992) and *Symposium of Rebirth* (1994).

ALTAR

Guaranteed to get right up the noses of Christians, this Dutch black-metal band claimed on their website that they were 'virtual outcasts in their hometowns Hardenberg and Coevorden'.

Certainly, their underground demo, 'And God Created Satan to Blame for his Mistakes', can't have endeared them to the local church elders.

Their albums are thought of as 'brutal', and include *Youth Against Christ* (1994) and *In the Name of the Father* (1999).

ANATHEMA

A slow and detuned sound is the hallmark of this British doom-metal band, who comprise Vincent Cavanagh on guitar and vocals, Daniel Cavanagh on guitar, Martin Powel on keyboards and violin, Dave Pybus on bass and Sean Steels on drums.

Probably the British metal fans' fondness for the heaviness of seventies bands such as Black Sabbath is one reason for the success of Anathema, whose albums include *Serenades* (1993), *The Silent Enigma* (1995) and *Judgement* (1999).

ANGEL CORPSE

Wonderful name. This is a death-metal outfit from the States, formed in 1995 by Gene Palubicki and Pete Helmkamp.

They toured extensively to promote their album *Hammer of Gods*, and have played major shows such as the Milwaukee Metalfest. Another album followed, the aggressive *Exterminate*.

ANTHRAX

Very influential in the 1980s as a thrash band, they were founded by the guitarist Scott Ian. The band's name came about, so it is said, during a biology course.

Ian recruited Charlie Benante on drums, Dan Lilker on bass, Greg Walls on lead guitar and Neil Turbin on vocals, and their debut album was *Fistful of Metal*, recorded in 1983 (you'll remember the sleeve if you're a fan: it was a picture of a fist bursting out of a metaller's mouth – and it was badly drawn, too).

There were changes in the line-up after this album, and a singer who rejoices in the name of Joey Belladonna joined up, and brought with him a tremendous vocal range. All good things must come to an end, and Belladonna eventually left the band, which showed in their 1993 album *Sound of White Noise*. It just wasn't Anthrax any more, said some.

Among this band's albums are also to be found *Among the Living* (1987), *Attack of the Killer B's* (1991), *Stomp 442* (1995) and *Return of the Killer A's* (1999).

ATHEIST

This outfit from Florida were into thrash metal but evolved into death metal, and recorded three successful albums. The founder member of the band – and its linchpin – was Roger Patterson, who died in 1991, and the band split in 1993.

The three albums they released were *Piece of Time* (1989), *Unquestionable Presence* (1991) and *Elements* (1993).

BAL-SAGOTH

Funny and well known among British bands, Bal-Sagoth specialize in a rather slow riffing and are noted for their rather eccentric singer Byron.

He formed the band in 1993 to concentrate on fantasy, science fiction and mythology. They became recognized among fans of doom after their album *A Black Moon Broods Over Lemuria* in 1995, which was followed up in 1996 with *Starfire Burning Upon the Ice-Veiled Throne of Ultima Thule*.

Byron started to experiment with war themes on the next album, *Battle Magic*.

BATHORY

This Swedish outfit were black metal first, but then became one of the pioneers of Viking metal, though they've been dubbed both death and thrash, because there are elements of these subgenres in their style.

They released an eponymous album in 1984 and soon got a cult following that has stayed with them over the years.

Much of their success is down to the shadowy band member Quorthon, who rarely goes to media dos and is a self-styled mystery.

Demonic subjects litter Quorthon's lyrics, and his genius is often referred to by other bands (such as Emperor). Some of Bathory's albums were recorded in a 'studio' that doubled as a storeroom and garage, resulting in a less-than-perfect production. However, Quorthon was surprised to learn that his fans rather liked this.

His fans, it seems, like him to remain a mystery and were a bit miffed when, in the mid-nineties, he told too much about himself on a sleeve note.

Satanic themes eventually gave way to the mythology closer to home (after all, Satan is a Christian invention), and Quorthon used Nordic mythology for his inspiration. Three albums that epitomize this are *Blood Fire Death* (1989), *Hammerheart* (1990) and *Twilight of the Gods* (1991). Quorthon has said that the band is really a hobby, and he's been amazed by the loyalty of his fans. The band takes its name from Elizabeth, Countess Bathory, a sixteenth-century Hungarian aristocrat of legendary beauty who allegedly murdered more than six hundred young girls and bathed in their blood, believing that this would keep her youthful. Sometimes known as 'Countess Dracula', she was sentenced to life imprisonment walled up within her own castle.

BENEDICTION

This Birmingham (UK) band have been one of the best among the death-metal fraternity. Their first album was *Subconscious Terror* in 1989, when they featured the sometime vocalist with Napalm Death, Barney Greenway.

They're known for a terrific live show on stage and have had especially successful appearances with the likes of Bolt Thrower, Autopsy and Paradise Lost, and among their classic albums are *Return to the Eve* (1992) and *The Dreams You Dread* (1995).

BLACK SABBATH

To many, Black Sabbath *are* heavy metal, and doom metallers have used the Sabs' heavy, slow and gloomy chords as their influence – among them My Dying Bride, Beseech, Anathema and Acrimony.

The first six Sabbath albums are regarded as their very best, and they all used the slow grind of their first efforts.

There's a story about the guitarist Tony Iommi, who lost the tips of his fingers. He tuned down his guitar a semitone, because this made the strings a little slacker and therefore more comfortable. The resultant sound came as something new and innovative in the seventies.

Drugs, madness, black magic, the occult and suicide peppered their lyrics, and Black Sabbath are among the all-time great metal bands for their powerful playing.

They once had Ozzy Osbourne, of course, but he left the band in 1979, and was replaced by Ronnie James Dio. The first album featuring Dio was *Heaven and Hell*. His vocal style wasn't welcomed by all Black Sabbath fans.

There have been a number of reunion concerts, though, featuring Ozzy Osbourne, and many heavy-metal bands the world over can claim the influence of the legendary Black Sabbath.

Body Count

A different sort of black metal, this, because all the members are black, and include the gangsta-rap star Ice-T on vocals. To have an all-black line-up among heavy-metal bands is a rarity.

They all met up at high school in Los Angeles and remained friends as Ice-T shot to fame in the early nineties when he was TV personality, political commentator and rapper all in one.

Ice-T has made no secret of the fact that he's used Body Count as a vehicle for his political views and anti-racist campaigning. In 1992, the lead single on the band's *Body Count* album was called 'There Goes the Neighborhood', and contained lines such as 'Here come those fuckin' niggers/With their fancy cars!'; and there was also a song called 'KKK Bitch'.

Bolt Thrower

The name sounds more Scandinavian, summoning up visions of Thor the thunder god, but they're a British extreme-metal band, and are one of the best known. Although their roots are in eighties thrash metal, their style became that of death metal.

Bolt Thrower were formed in 1986, and in the early nineties were snapped up by the Radio 1 disc jockey John Peel, who used them in his *Peel Sessions* series, recording an album with them.

The band's themes are warlike (a bolt thrower delivers not so much a bolt of lightning as the sort of arrow – a bolt – that you get in a crossbow), and you can see this in album titles such as *In Battle There Is No Law* (1988), *Warmaster* (1991) and *Mercenary* (1998).

BON JOVI

This New Jersey band have the rare distinction of having been voted, in the annual readers' poll that appears in the UK metal magazine *Kerrang!*, best band and best album (for *These Days*) and, oddly enough, worst band and worst album (for *These Days*)!

The man who gave his name to the band is of course Jon Bon Jovi (although he was born John Francis Bongiovi Jr in March 1962). Bongiovi met future band member David Bryan (David Rashbaum) in high school, where they shared an interest in rock music.

Bongiovi and Bryan eventually moved to New York (Bryan went to study music, and Bongiovi followed), and a demo tape was recorded with the connivance of Bongiovi's cousin, who owned a studio. One track, 'Runaway', was played on local radio and appeared on a local artist's compilation album.

By 1983, a line-up had been established and the

band Bon Jovi had a recording contract with PolyGram, and were doing support acts for Eddie Money and ZZ Top. Jon Bon Jovi turned down a chance to appear in the Kevin Bacon dance movie *Footloose* because he was too wrapped up in his music and wanted to pursue that in preference to anything else.

Their debut album was called *Bon Jovi* (1984), and was followed in 1985 by *7800 Degrees Fahrenheit*, which met only cynicism from the music journalists, who didn't seem to like the band's rather manicured image. It was, anyway, a rather lacklustre album.

But they came back with a vengeance, and their third effort, *Slippery When Wet* (1986), was the biggest-selling album of 1987. Because of a collaboration with the songwriter Desmond Child, three tracks from the album, 'Wanted Dead or Alive', 'You Give Love a Bad Name' and 'Livin' on a Prayer', were big hits in both Europe and the United States.

New Jersey was their fourth album, which was issued in 1988. It was around this time that Bon Jovi were headlining the Monsters of Rock shows in Europe.

More touring ensued in 1989, and then the band went into hibernation. Jon Bon Jovi said at the time that he wanted to 'ride my bike into the hills, learn how to garden, anything except do another Bon Jovi record'. He began a solo career instead, which saw him star in the film *Young Guns II* and record a quasi-soundtrack of some of the music from the film, which gave him his first solo album, in 1990.

However, Bon Jovi were back together for *Keep the Faith*, released in 1992, and other albums followed for this highly successful band, notable among them being *These Days* (1995), *Crush* (2000) and *One Wild Night: Live 1985–2001* (2001).

BURZUM

This band have similarities to Bathory in two ways: one is that they share some musical and thematic characteristics; the other is that they're the work, to all intents and purposes, of one man. The man in this case is Varg Vikernes, a Norwegian who's also known by a stage name or *nom de guerre*, Count Grishnackh (two names from J. R. R. Tolkien's *The Lord of the Rings* trilogy).

Vikernes played in death-metal bands in the eighties, and then became involved with a group of Satanists called the Inner Circle, whose leader was called Euronymous, although his real name was Øystein Aarseth, who, as well as owning a record label called Death, also owned a record shop whose name in English is Hell.

Euronymous was also the guitarist with the band Mayhem, whose singer, Per Yngve Ohlin, known professionally as Dead, had . . . well, died. He'd committed suicide by slitting his wrists and then blowing his brains out, and one story has it that Euronymous cooked bits of his brain and ate them before informing the police of his discovery of the corpse. Another story says that he and the Mayhem drummer Hellhammer (Jan Axel von Blomberg) both discovered the body, photographed it and took bits of the skull and stuck them on necklaces.

But back to Vikernes. Euronymous was so impressed by him that he asked him to play bass guitar in a Mayhem album. After burning some churches (as was his wont), Vikernes was arrested, but was released because the prosecution couldn't amass enough strong evidence.

Burzum was beginning by now to gain recognition, and this led to tensions between Euronymous and Vikernes, and the latter murdered the former by stabbing him to death in 1993. He's currently serving a twenty-one year jail term.

Vikernes has always been fascinated by the works of Tolkien and with legends and folk myths in particular. He thinks Judeo-Christian beliefs should be replaced with the religious system of yore, and with the social structure of those ancient times, too.

Until Vikernes's enforced departure from the band, Burzum was a controversial and very black black-metal band: lots of screams and fast riffs. He began issuing albums from jail, but was not allowed to use guitars (potential weapons, presumably), and so produced material that was keyboard-based. Among notable albums have been *Burzum* (1991), *Filosofem* (1995) and *Hlidskjalf* (1999).

CANDLEMASS

The 'new' Black Sabbath? Some would say so. They've been described as second only to, and this Swedish outfit have been responsible for most of the detuned, sludgy and slow stuff that currently goes under the name of 'doom'.

The line-up has changed over the years, but their founder in 1985 was the bassist Leif Edling, who had played with Nemesis. They achieved immediate following after their first album, *Epicus Doomicus Metallicus*, in 1986, and some notable albums since then have been *Tales of Creation* (1989), *As It Is, As It Was* (1994) and *From the 13th Sun* (1999). Their inability to grasp mainstream success is largely down to their sticking to the doom format, a style they haven't deviated from.

The band have never achieved their glory days since Edling left to found an outfit called Abstrakt Algebra.

CATHEDRAL

Another noted doom band, this time from the UK, are Cathedral, formed by Lee Dorrian, formerly singer with Napalm Death. He formed Cathedral in 1990 with Gary Jennings and Adam Lehan on guitars, Ben Mochrie on drums and Mark Griffiths on bass.

They had a style that owed much to Black Sabbath, and mixed it with seventies psychedelia, evidenced on their 1991 EP *In Memorium* and their first album, *Forest of Equilibrium*.

Like many bands, they had line-up changes, and brought out two more albums in the mid-nineties, *The Carnival Bizarre* and *Supernatural Birth*. Also notable among their albums have been *Caravan Beyond Redemption* (1999) and *Endtyme* (2001).

CEMETARY

Yes, with an 'a'. This was a Swedish band who spanned a six-year career after beginning as death with *An Evil Shade of Grey* in 1992. However, they took doom and trad metal into their repertoire on subsequent works, and gothic doom was there with *Last Confession* (1997).

One of the band's founders, the singer-guitarist Maṭhias Lodmalm, disbanded the outfit in 1997. He thought Cemetary had done all they needed to do and could go no further.

CORONER

Another band to quit while they were doing well were the Swiss outfit Coroner, founded in 1985, with Ron Royce on bass and vocals, Marquis Marky on drums and Tommy T. Baron on guitar.

Black-metal and death-metal veined what was a mainly avant-garde thrash-metal style. Indeed, *R.I.P.* in 1987 was reminiscent of the death style and themes of Coroner.

The band had a stage show that was high on theatrics, and so attracted an immediate fan following.

Punishment for Decadence and *No More Color* (1988 and 1989 respectively) were very death in style. The band toured with such acts as Motörhead and Watchtower, and frequently appeared on MTV.

The band seemed to be in a bit of a rut by the early nineties, as evidenced by the laid-back 1993 album *Grin*, and the outfit disbanded in 1994, before their last album, *Coroner*, was released in 1995.

DARK ANGEL

Another UK band that showed great technical proficiency in the thrash department, Dark Angel displayed similarities to Metallica and Slayer.

Their line-up was quite fluid, with different band members taking on various roles at various times.

Time Does Not Heal (1991) is regarded as Dark Angel's best work (it even had a sticker on it saying there were 246 riffs in the album's contents).

They disbanded in 1992, but are up there with Slayer and Annihilator as a great exponent of speed metal.

DARKTHRONE

This Oslo band originally performed under the name Black Death in 1986, and are, appropriately, one of the world's best black-metal outfits. The name was changed to Darkthrone in 1988. Songs from demos were included in their debut album, *Soulside Journey*, recorded in Stockholm in 1990.

Influences for some later material can be found in Mayhem and Bathory, among others. This was evident on the album *Goatlord*, on which the Satyricon singer Satyr guested. However, it was not released until 1997, issued by Moonfog, the label to which the band had signed (run by Sigurd Wongraven, alias the aforementioned Satyr, of Satyricon).

Back to the early nineties, however, and Darkthrone's classic *A Blaze in the Northern Sky* was released in 1991. By now they'd begun to use corpse paint and stage names such as Fenriz, Nocturno Culto and Zephyrous.

Fenriz (alias Gylve Nagell, one of Black Death's founders) is quoted as saying the band died after *Soulside Journey* and fans agree that the outfit fits neatly into two distinct phases. The 'new' Darkthrone came after that album, and their aggressive black-metal style is evident in *Under a Funeral Moon* (1993). Indeed, the sleeve notes carried the legend 'True Norwegian black metal'.

One of the band's albums, *Transilvanian Hunger*, is supposed to have taken its title from the suicide of the Mayhem singer, Dead, who was wearing a shirt at the time with 'I Love Transilvania' printed on it (see the entries for Burzum and Mayhem). Count Grishnackh (alias Varg Vikernes of Burzum) wrote many of the lyrics, including the backwards-way-on message at the end of one of the songs saying, 'In the name of God, let the churches burn.'

There was something of a hiatus between 1996 and 1999, which has never been adequately explained. Notable among their albums are also *Total Death* (1996) and *Ravishing Grimness* (1999).

DEATH

This outfit was arguably the world's most influential in its chosen subgenre, predictably death metal. While central to the band was the guitarist-singer Chuck Schuldiner (who had formed Mantas in 1983), there were several changes to the line-up.

Noted for complex, highly technical riffing, Death have influenced a number of subsequent bands between the late eighties and mid-nineties.

Death signed up to the Combat label, and the debut album was *Scream Bloody Gore*, released in 1987 – a classic no death metaller would be without.

More albums followed in the next few years, all displaying technical progress, but they seemed to get into a rut in 1995, when *Symbolic* was released.

They were also a well-travelled outfit, having made tours of Asia, Europe and the Americas. They disbanded in the mid-nineties.

Other albums include *Spiritual Healing* (1990) and *Sound of Perseverance* (1998).

DEEP PURPLE

Wailing vocals and very long guitar solos are what characterized Deep Purple. This band formed in the same year as Led Zeppelin, 1968, and the wailing voice and guitar solos were, respectively, the work of

Ian Gillan and Ritchie Blackmore. Making up the line-up were Jon Lord on keyboards, Roger Glover on bass and Ian Paice on drums.

'Extravagant' is a word that comes to mind when one recalls the playing style of all the musicians in the band, developing the form and pushing at the edges to create something unique. Classical influence was to be found in their music too, and, in 1970, they recorded *Concerto for Group and Orchestra*, in collaboration with the English composer, trumpeter and conductor Malcolm Arnold.

Their album *Deep Purple in Rock* also came in 1970, establishing the distinctive style of the band. *Fireball* came out in 1971, followed in 1972 by *Machine Head*, and *Made in Japan* was released in 1973. They were all widely popular pieces of work.

A single that became big in the States, 'Smoke on the Water', is still dubbed a classic.

Deep Purple broke up in 1976 after some changes to the line-up, but re-formed eight years later. A hard sound and a flamboyance of style are two of the hallmarks of Deep Purple, emulated by heavy-metal bands today.

DEICIDE

These Florida guys, who originally performed under the name Amon, really mean it when they say they have satanic beliefs. Their brutal death-metal style combines with satanic lyrics, and they're among the leaders of the death scene – up there with the likes of Obituary and Morbid Angel.

Glen Benton is at the centre of things, and has made some controversial statements over the years which have caused comment, not least from animal-rights protesters. Hardly surprising when they strut onto the stage in spiky 'god' armour, covered in pig's blood and throwing pieces of meat into the audience.

Benton is supposed to have advocated animal torture – something guaranteed to get up the noses of animal lovers (in fact, up the nose of anyone with an ounce of rationalism and compassion for fellow creatures).

Benton has protested his innocence of animal hatred, by telling the world he owns a dachshund – as a pet, not an unwilling S&M partner. Benton has a young son (aged about twelve at the time of writing) – and he's called Daemon!

A couple of notable albums from this band are *Amon: Feasting the Beast* (1993) and *Serpents of the Light* (1997).

DISINCARNATE

James Murphy, this band's guitarist, has also played with Death, Obituary, Testament and Cancer, and is a gifted musician and writer.

His musicianship is to be found in Death's *Spiritual Healing* album. Disincarnate produced only one album – *Reams of the Carrion Kind* in 1993.

ENTOMBED

This outfit is a huge Swedish band, whose members' musical partnership goes back to 1987, when some were in a band called Nihilist. Entombed's *Left Hand Path* (1990) is seen as a classic in death-metal circles, and other notable works have been *Wolverine Blues* (1993), *Entombed* (1997) and *Uprising* (2000).

The band's singer, Lars-Goran Petrov (known as L-G), left them for a year, but returned, and their next album, *Clandestine*, was highly successful, as was *Wolverine Blues*, which made them truly international and was voted second-best record of 1993 by *Kerrang!*, the magazine of the heavy-metal world.

The media coined the term 'death 'n' roll' for the band's mixture of trad rock and metal, and Entombed were seen to have gone mainstream by the late nineties.

Exodus

When Dave Mustaine left Metallica, the singer and lead guitarist with Exodus, Kirk Hammett, joined them in 1983. Exodus bemoaned this, but still managed to be a well-respected speed-metal band.

In fact, Hammett had been gone two years before the band's first album, *Bonded By Blood*, came out in 1985.

There were six more albums, majoring on the band's plodding speed-metal style, before the outfit disbanded in 1992. They tried a return in 1996 and a new live album of old songs was released, but it amounted to nothing. Notable albums include *Good Friendly Violent Fun* (1991), *Lessons In Violence* (1992) and *Force of Habit* (1992).

Fleshcrawl

Much underground praise followed this band's debut work *Descend Into the Absurd* in 1992, which came after a series of successful demo tapes. They began to tour extensively after a second album, *Impurity* (1994), and began a business relationship with the death-metal producer Peter Tägtgren, when they produced *Bloodsoul* – vicious stuff that went down well with death fans.

There was more touring, and a fourth album,

Bloodred Massacre, recorded over just two weeks in 1997, which contained a cover version of Slayer's 'Necrophiliac'. Another album of note from this outfit is 2000's *The Path of Endless Fire*.

GODDESS OF DESIRE

Three scantily-dressed young women are part of this Dutch band's elaborate stage presence, each with a predictable name: Lilith, Delilah and Medusa. The band came together in 1995 and played cover versions of music by such bands as Slayer and Kreator.

They used trad-metal structures and some thrash riffs on their 1998 album, *Let Us Win This War*, and issued a picture disc called *Let Us Win This War II*.

If you were at the Wacken festival you'll no doubt have the 1999 video *Alive At Wacken*, an occasion on which six strippers were used and the bassist-vocalist Count August threw a hundred litres of beer into the audience.

HADES

This band found it difficult to stay together, such was the internal tension among members (Alan Tecchio on vocals, Ed Fuhrman and Dan Lorenzo on guitars,

Scott LePage on bass and Dave Lescinsky on drums). The band finally split in 1989 after a long European tour, with Tecchio and Lorenzo founding a band called Non Fiction. They occasionally performed Hades reunion concerts.

While they were an item, this American thrash band released a song on the compilation album *Metal Massacre VI* and followed it with their own *Resisting Success* and *If At First You Don't Succeed*.

The band members come together for occasional recordings, following *SaviorSelf* in 1998. Other notable albums have been *Live On Location* (1992) and *Exist To Resist* (1996).

HELLOWEEN

This Hamburg band are said to be the inventors of power metal, and among their heroes are Iron Maiden, which shows in their early material.

The four members – Kai Hansen (guitar), Michael Weikath (guitar), Marcus Grosskopf (bass) and Ingo Schwichtenberg (drums) – had been together before Helloween, since 1982, in fact, in a band called Iron Fist.

Their first album was *Walls of Jericho*, which came out in 1985, and this was followed two years later by *Keeper of the Seven Keys Part I* (*Part II* was to follow in 1988).

They have a clean and fast formula with occasional humour (as in the 1991 album *Pink Bubbles Go Ape*).

Another notable work is *Metal Jukebox* (1999), which is made up of cover versions of other bands' songs.

ICED EARTH

This American band, formed in 1987 – but then called Purgatory – are among the very best of power-metal outfits, and were based in Florida until 1997. They then moved to Indiana and became established as a powerful underground act.

The album widely thought to have made the band's name is *The Dark Saga*, which came out in 1996. In 1997, the band released *Days of Purgatory*, comprising songs from their *Iced Earth* (1991) and *Night of the Stormrider* (1992).

They incorporated acoustic guitar and woodwind into *Something Wicked This Way Comes* (1998), and featured a conceptual piece lasting twenty minutes.

INCANTATION

This band began in 1989, formed by John McEntee, their guitarist, who's been their most constant member.

The outfit released *Onward to Golgotha*, their debut, in 1992, and followed this up in 1994 with *Mortal Throne of Nazarene*, which was the last album recorded by the original line-up.

John McEntee took on three musicians for tours, and a third album, *Upon the Throne of Apocalypse* – a limited-edition version of *Mortal Throne of Nazarene* – came out in 1995.

Incantation toured with Anal Cunt and recorded a live album called *Tribute to the Goat*, released in 1997.

INTERNAL BLEEDING

Internal Bleeding, an extreme American death-metal band, was formed in 1991 with Chris Pervelis in the driving seat (he'd been a guitarist with the doom-metal outfit Autumn Reign).

Before establishing a committed line-up they released two albums, *Voracious Contempt* (1995) and *The Extinction of Benevolence* (1997).

IRON MAIDEN

This band were formed by Steve Harris in 1975. He'd got the name from the horrific metal coffin with spikes inside that he'd seen on an old version of the film *The Man in the Iron Mask*.

The band gigged in Stratford in east London and were soon getting gigs in other parts of the capital, too. Before long, after some falling out and line-up changes, the band had a fair old following, and came to the attention of EMI records, for whom they signed.

They were featured in the music paper *Sounds*, in a feature written by Geoff Barton, the man who coined the phrase 'the new wave of British heavy metal' (NWOBHM). Barton went on to found the leading heavy-metal paper *Kerrang!*.

After an EP and some singles for a compilation album, *Metal for Muthas*, Maiden eventually appeared on BBC television's *Top of the Pops* in 1980. This was on the strength of their single, 'Running Free'. In April that year, *Iron Maiden*, their debut album, was released and charted at Number 4.

Iron Maiden's turning-point album was their fifth, *Powerslave*, because some commentators say that, if there's a fold in the paper that tells the history of heavy metal, this is it. There's the music on one side of the fold, and what came after. And what came after was NWOBHM.

And this is where Iron Maiden are seen to have hit

their peak. It's a heavy album, but progressive and innovative, with a couple of tracks that beg for attention, 'Rime of the Ancient Mariner' and '2 Minutes to Midnight'.

Between the debut and this album, there had been *Killers* (1981), *The Number of the Beast* (1982) and *Piece of Mind* (1983).

The World Slavery Tour in 1985 (for the *Powerslave* album) saw Maiden play to their biggest-ever audience: 200,000 at the Rock in Rio Festival.

Band members have come and gone over the years (Maiden are noted for their fluid personnel), as tours have become more elaborate. They released *Brave New World* in 2000 and *Rock in Rio* in 2002.

JAG PANZER

This Colorado band are a power-metal outfit not dissimilar to Iced Earth, and named themselves after the German tank, the Jagdpanzer. They were formed in 1981 (as Tyrants) by Mark Briody (guitar), John Tetley (bass), Rick Hilyard (drums) and Harry Conklin (vocals). The Tyrants produced a mini-album, known as the *Tyrants* EP.

Jim Morris produced their nineties albums, but the album that gets the highest numbers of thumbs up is the 1984 work *Ample Destruction*.

They had some internal disagreements after that, and they were inactive for about ten years. There were line-up changes, and Conklin left to join an outfit called Titan Force. It was thought that Jag Panzer was a thing of the past, but out came *Dissident Alliance* in 1994, and then the band did a tour of Europe.

Other notable albums have been *The Fourth Judgement* (1997) and *Age of Mastery* (1998).

JUDAS PRIEST

First the name. It came about from their singer Alan Atkins's previous band, which had taken it from a Bob Dylan song, 'The Ballad of Frankie Lee and Judas Priest'.

Another British metal band, Priest, were formed in Birmingham in 1969 by K. K. (Kenneth) Dowling, who played guitar, and his friend Ian Hill (who played bass). Atkins completed their line-up, along with John Ellis on drums.

The band did a lot of gigging, and there were line-up changes, but they were attracting a faithful following, and by 1974 they were touring abroad for the first time, in Germany and the Netherlands.

That year also saw their album debut with *Rocka Rolla*, but they weren't too pleased with it, and it didn't have much impact.

The band's appearance at the Reading Festival in 1975 brought them to a much wider audience, and their next album, *Sad Wings of Destiny* (1977), was an improvement on *Rocka Rolla*. The band gained a worldwide contract with CBS Records, and *Sin After Sin* was recorded, and seen as a strong collection of tracks.

The USA was next on the band's agenda, and then came *Stained Glass* in 1978 and *Killing Machine* (1979), the latter giving Priest their first UK hit single, 'Take On The World'.

During the band's 1979 Japanese tour, they recorded *Unleashed in the East*, and the band gained even more popularity and following after tours with AC/DC and Kiss.

Album after album, and a number of line-up changes, marked the subsequent years, and Judas Priest were still a potent force in the music world. Among albums during the eighties were *Screaming for Vengeance*, *Defenders of the Faith*, *Priest Live* and *Ram It Down*, while notable among their releases in subsequent decades have been *Painkiller* (1990), *Jugulator* (1997), *Concert Classics* (1998) and *Meltdown '98 Live* (1998) and *Demolition* (2001). The DVD *Judas Priest – Live in London* was released in both the UK and the USA in July 2002.

Priest will be remembered even by non-aficionados as the band who were taken to court in 1990 for allegedly putting subliminal messages into their record tracks, after two fans had committed suicide in 1985. CBS were taken to court, too, and it wasn't until June 1993, after a long court battle, that the band and the company were cleared. K. K. Downing said at the time, 'It'll be another ten years before I can even *spell* subliminal!'

Judas Priest – as evidenced by the longer profile in this book – are one of the most enduring bands in the heavy-metal genre, known even to non-metalheads and widely respected throughout the music industry. At the time of going to press, they were entering the second leg of an extensive American tour during July and August 2002. They'll figure prominently in the annals for a long time.

KING DIAMOND

King Diamond (a former professional footballer) left Mercyful Fate in 1985 and formed a band called . . . well, King Diamond. In came Andy LaRocque and Herbie Simonsen on guitars, Chris Estes on bass and Darrin Anthony on drums, and songs dealing with occult themes ensued.

They introduced an unusual feature to their stage performances by using actors to play the characters in the songs.

Mercyful Fate got back together in 1993, and King

Diamond split his talents between both bands. Line-ups have changed over the years.

Among the notable albums to come from this band have been *Abigail* (1987), *Conspiracy* (1989), *A Dangerous Meeting* (1992) and *Voodoo* (1998).

KREATOR

Thrash (or speed – take your pick) is the forte of this German band, formed in 1983.

Mille Petrozza, their singer-guitarist, was the man around whom the band revolved, and more than a dozen albums have come from him and other musicians.

The band attracted the epithet 'hate metal' because Petrozza's voice is filled with fury and his guitar riffs are nothing if not angry.

Their milestone albums were the first: *Endless Pain* (1985) and *Pleasure To Kill* (1986), and the band brought more death-metal styles into their playing in subsequent albums.

But Petrozza didn't want to get into a rut, and the 1992 album *Renewal* incorporated industrial rock.

Other significant albums have been *Extreme Aggression* (1989), *Scenarios of Violence* (1996) and *Voices of Transgression* (1999).

LAKE OF TEARS

This Swedish band's debut album, *Greater Art* (1994), was co-produced by Mathias Lodmalm of Cemetary. Some of their later music was clearly influenced by the 1970s psychedelic style.

However, there were just too many influences preying on this talented outfit, and, feeling constricted, they went their separate ways in 1999, leaving fans with three further albums, *Headstones* (1995), *A Crimson Cosmos* (1997) and *Forever Autumn* (1999).

LED ZEPPELIN

Count Ferdinand von Zeppelin, he of First World War airship fame, remained blithely unaware that his name, fifty years after his death, would become adopted by the band that some say epitomizes early heavy metal. Led Zeppelin were formed in 1968 by Jimmy Page (guitar), Robert Plant (vocals), John Paul Jones (bass) and John Bonham (drums).

Of course, depending on whose version you read, Zeppelin were not heavy metal, but remained within the boundaries of the blues/rock tradition. Or they were progressive rock. One thing is certain, though: when metal is being discussed, their name crops up.

*'You see, here I am, the lead singer
with Led Zeppelin, and underneath
I still enjoy people like
Fairport Convention and
Buffalo Springfield.
Some people may find
that surprising.'*

ROBERT PLANT, Led Zeppelin

What characterized their music was a blues-based guitar style, already familiar to music lovers in the sixties – but this was altogether more aggressive, more wild and loud as hell (but not nearly so loud as metal was to become in its more ferocious, raw, pummelling, brutal and warp-speed incarnations).

The sixties is a decade associated in the popular mind with easy-listening music such as some of The Beatles' earlier songs and all those groups that made it into the Top Ten: The Hollies, The Searchers, The Bachelors and so on. However, it must be must remembered that what we called rock and roll in the sixties was a largely watered-down version of what many saw as the real thing, and the era of rock and roll – *true* rock and roll – is seen as ending at around 1959.

Zeppelin were seen by many to have turned rock music in a new direction, and heavy metal was born, although it's never easy to pin a label on one particular form of music and say, 'This is where it started.' It may be more accurate to say that their brand of rock music provided a seminal moment – or even a semi-seminal moment!

Their first album, called simply *Led Zeppelin*, came out in 1969 and, not to be outdone in the Imaginative Album Titles Awards, the band brought out *Led Zeppelin II* that same year and *Led Zeppelin III* in 1970.

What Zeppelin released in 1971 was popularly called *Zoso*, otherwise known as *Led Zeppelin IV*, but it was untitled (*Zoso* comes from some cryptic characters on the album cover). It was around this time that the band's music softened somewhat, rather influenced by the occult and folk music.

John Bonham died from an alcohol overdose in 1980, and the band broke up. Page released a solo album and Plant, too, developed a solo career. Page went on to release another album as a member of Coverdale Page, a hard-rock duo, in 1993.

Bonham's son Jason took on his father's role in a reunion concert in 1988, which marked the fortieth anniversary of the founding of the band's record company, Atlantic Records.

Led Zeppelin are still seen as a major influence on rock music, and that influence has spread to one of the form's later incarnations, grunge, which developed in the early 1990s as another guitar-based style of rock music. In 1995 the band were inducted into the Rock and Roll Hall of Fame.

'I get hell for going on tour.
Once I had all the time in the
world and no money.
Now I have the money
but no time.'

JOHN PAUL JONES, Led Zeppelin

LIFE OF AGONY

This New York band were destined for success right after their debut album, *River Runs Red* in 1991. The band (Keith Caputo on vocals, Alan Robert on bass, Joey Z on guitar and, later, Sal Abruscato on drums) toured extensively to promote the debut work with a number of well known acts, including Britain's own Ozzy Osbourne.

The band's follow-up album in 1995 was *Ugly*, but this displeased fans, who saw it as moving too close to rock. This work was followed two years later by *Soul*

Searching Sun, which got no better reception than *Ugly*. The band split in 1999, and a 'best of' album, *Life of Agony 1989–1999* was released in 2000.

LIMP BIZKIT

It all began in a tattoo parlour run by Fred Durst, Limp Bizkit's singer, when two members of the band Korn were touring Florida, and went for tattoos. A friendship was struck up, and Durst eventually gave the guys a copy of Bizkit's demo, which Korn's producer liked.

Soon, Bizkit were touring with two other bands, the Deftones and House of Pain. They eventually signed to Flip records and released their debut album *'Three Dollar Bill Y'All$*, in 1997. This caught the imagination of rock fans on MTV and went on to notch up huge sales.

This hard-rock/hip-hop band also have a terrific stage show, with garish backdrops and breakdancers, and their stagemanship and musicianship have earned them places in big festivals, including Ozzfest.

Durst went on to make guest appearances on other bands' albums, and became an A&R man for his own record label, Flip.

Bizkit brought out *Significant Other* in 1999, and it topped the US chart, confirming the outfit as a force to be reckoned with. The following year, they recorded 'Take A Look Around', the theme song on the Tom Cruise film, *Mission: Impossible 2*.

The band spearheaded the breakthrough of so-called 'nu-metal' in Europe with a song called 'Rollin'', which topped the UK singles chart for a couple of weeks in January 2001.

Other notable albums have been *Chocolate Starfish and the Hot Dog Flavored Water* (2000) and *The Interview Sessions*.

THE LORD WIERD SLOUGH FEG

Weird they certainly are, including that misspelling of 'weird' in their name. A bit on the avant-garde side, they became known as the Fegs and played what they called 'Slough Feg music', a label that prevented their being categorized as playing any other kind of music.

Influences from Queen and Black Sabbath can be detected as well as other heavy-metal foundations.

Lobbing meat into the audience is one of this outfit's party pieces, as well as burning torches on stage while dolled up as witches.

Notable albums include *The Lord Wierd Slough Feg* and *Twilight of the Idols* (1998 and 1999 respectively).

MACHINE HEAD

Detuned riffing with a dash of eighties thrash characterize the style of this San Francisco band.

They were formed in 1992 by the guitarist-vocalist Rob Flynn, and toured with bands such as Pantera, Marilyn Manson and Megadeth, and appeared at the 1997 Ozzfest with Black Sabbath.

Guttural vocal emanations from Flynn combined with very heavy guitar helped to create Machine Head's identifying sound.

Their second album, in 1997, was *The More Things Change . . .*, and this was followed by *The Burning Red* in 1999.

MARDUK

This is one of the most successful black-metal bands to come out of Sweden (Bathory are probably the most famous). They were put together in 1990 by Morgan Hakansson, and have a plethora of albums to their name, with some wonderful titles, too: *Those of the Unlight* (1993), *Fuck Me Jesus* (a mini-album, 1995), *Heaven Shall Burn . . . When We Are Gathered* (1996) and *Nightwing* (1998).

The second of these – exemplifying Marduk's anti-Christian message – was banned in seven countries because the sleeve showed a woman masturbating with a crucifix.

Another band who wear corpse paint, Marduk are known for great musicianship. Marduk supported Mayhem at the latter's London concert in 1999.

MARILYN MANSON

Marilyn Manson's real name is Brian Warner (born in 1969 in Ohio), and this band, which was formed to test 'the limits of censorship', came together in 1989 as Marilyn Manson & the Spooky Kids. Very much an industrial-rock outfit, its members took the names of female icons or murderers: Daisy Berkowitz, for instance, and Olivia Newton-Bundy.

The funniest [gig] was when a guy in New Jersey told us we couldn't play because we were not suitable for the local community and if we didn't like it we could sue them. So we did and we won.

MARILYN MANSON, June 1997

Full marks to them for setting out to offend right-wing Christians, but they upset a number of other people, too, and Manson had to defend himself morally when a couple of deranged alleged 'fans' decided it would be a good idea to murder fifteen of their school pals in the notorious Colombine High School massacre of 1998. The band abandoned a nationwide tour.

However, to go back a bit, the band's debut album, *Portrait of an American Family* (1994) had half its tracks mixed at the house where the infamous Tate murders took place (Nine Inch Nails have recorded there, too).

Manson addressed some of the issues raised by the Colombine school shootings on the album *Holly Wood (In the Shadow of the Valley of Death)*. Other notable albums have been *Smells Like Children* (1995), *Mechanical Animals* (1998) and *In The Spotlight With Marilyn Manson* (bonus extended CD).

MAYHEM

This Norwegian band are another of the big-verging-on-huge names of black metal, having taken their name (or so it is said) from the Venom song 'Mayhem With Mercy'.

Øystein Aarseth (guitar), a.k.a. Euronymous (see entry for Burzum), formed Mayhem in 1984, and their first album (after a couple of demos using a session singer from Messiah) was *Deathcrush* (1987), using the voice of Sven Erik Kristiansen (whose stage name is Maniac and who likes to cut himself on stage).

Their live album *Live in Leipzig* followed in 1993 and was re-released in 1994 and 1996.

Things took a turn for the worse when Dead (a.k.a. Per Yngve Ohlin) slashed his wrists and shot himself through the head, thus living – or dying – up to his chosen name. The body was discovered by Euronymous and the band's drummer Hellhammer (Jan Axel von Blomberg), who photographed it before they told the police of their find. The pictures were subsequently used on Mayhem artwork.

Euronymous himself was murdered outside his apartment in 1993 by Varg Vikernes, the man at the centre of Burzum. He's serving a jail term and has claimed the stabbing was carried out in self-defence.

The workaday running of the band fell into the hands of Hellhammer, who took on a new guitarist and brought back two members who'd earlier left the band, Necrobutcher (Jorn Stubberud) and Maniac.

A couple of other notable albums from this outfit are *De Mysteriis Dom Sathanas* (1994) and *Out from the Dark* (1996).

MEGADETH

Dave Mustaine (guitar, vocals) formed this best-known of speed-metal bands in 1983, and they rank along with Metallica, Slayer and Anthrax among the best thrash bands of the 1980s.

Mustaine was outspoken – and that's putting it mildly. He has often slated other bands and his rather aggressive stance has often been put down to an unfortunate childhood (with an uncaring mother) and subsequent drugs and alcohol habits.

Mustaine is also known for his formation of Metallica in 1981 with Lars Ulrich and James Hetfield, but he left after internal rows over his drugs habit and a fist fight with Hetfield after Hetfield had kicked Mustaine's dog.

Megadeth's debut album was *Killing Is My Business . . . And Business Is Good!* in 1985, which was followed in 1986 by *Peace Sells . . . But Who's Buying*.

Mustaine went into rehab in 1990 after he was arrested for a drink-driving offence. He managed to clean himself up.

He was injured in January 2002 and suffered serious nerve damage to his left arm and hand. The band then disbanded after nearly twenty years together. As we write this, Mustaine is considering his future projects.

Mustaine wrote on the band's website, 'In closing I would like to depart with the beautiful French words

I wrote on the record "Youthanasia": "*A tout le monde, à tous mes amis, Je vous aime, Je dois partir.*" (To all the world, to all my friends. I love you, I have to leave.)'

Albums over the years have included *Rust In Peace* (199), *Cryptic Writings* (1997) and *Risk* (1999).

MERCYFUL FATE

King Diamond's extraordinary singing style – operatic, soaring – helped to distinguish this Danish black-metal band, who were formed in the mid-eighties.

While lyrics concerned evil and the supernatural, thrash was the accompaniment, and some dextrous musicianship from Hank Shermann and Michael on guitars, the bassist Timi Hansen and Kim Ruzz on drums set this outfit on the golden – well, black – road to success.

After just two albums, however, they disbanded after internal rows, and Diamond went on to form King Diamond. Mercyful Fate re-formed in 1993, and more albums ensued in the nineties, which saw a number of line-up changes. Among the albums were *In the Shadows* (1993) and *9* (1999).

METALLICA

This San Francisco foursome have been the subject of many books, and remain as innovative as ever. Their thrash-metal days were really in the eighties (they've since gone on to a smoother style).

Lars Ulrich, Metallica's drummer, is an art-lover who almost went pro as a tennis player. This Dane from California was a teenager when Metallica began. After meeting James Hetfield through a newspaper ad, he then recruited a bassist, Ron McGovney. Dave Mustaine was soon added as guitarist, and then there were four.

Eventually, however, McGovney got his marching orders because the rest of the band didn't get on with him, and Cliff Burton of Trauma was recruited – with the proviso that Metallica relocate to San Francisco.

Mustaine left the band in 1983 after some disagreements and went on to form Megadeth. Kirk Hammett, founder of Exodus, came in to replace him, and the first album, *Kill 'Em All*, was released that year.

What characterized Metallica and electrified their fans were, among other things, the technical excellence and the vigorous and spirited playing of Ulrich on drums, with his pair of bass pedals, and Hetfield, with superfast chords. This was thrash metal at its best. *Kill 'Em All* was the inspiration for a number of other thrash-metal bands following them.

While the next album, *Ride the Lightning* (1984),

was different in many ways (an acoustic guitar was featured, and so was a ballad, 'Fade To Black'), it was still not sparing of the speed.

Sales of these two albums were astronomical, and placed the band firmly in the public spotlight. And fans of speed were not let down when their next album, *Master of Puppets*, came out in 1986. Indeed, many fans say it's not only Metallica's best, but *the* best in the world of metal.

'I think they [Metallica] used to be a band that personified rebellion and real metal that never got radio airplay and did not need it to be huge. Now they wear a different uniform as good little soldiers of the big players in Hollywood. It must be worth it: they are counting every single penny nowadays. I tell you what: if 235,000 people download Flotsam this year on Napster I promise I won't get mad.'

**JASON WARD of Flotsam and Jetsam
(from Metal Sludge website)**

There were tours, of course, with the likes of Ozzy Osbourne and Anthrax, but then tragedy struck when Cliff Burton was killed in a bus crash.

Jason Newsted of the band Flotsam and Jetsam came in, and *Garage Days Re-Revisited: The $5.98 EP* was issued. The band appeared at Donington in 1988.

Metallica moved away from thrash and more into mainstream rock. Their *Metallica* album (1991) has sold more than 15 million copies. Other notable albums have been *Live Shit: Binge & Purge* (1994), *Garage Inc.* (1998) and *S&M* (1999).

MY DYING BRIDE

Calvin Robertshaw on guitar, Aaron Stainthorpe on vocals, Rick Miah on drums and Andy Craighan on guitar formed this outfit in 1990, and they became one of the UK's biggest doom bands.

Ade Jackson came in to play bass on three EPs and the band's first album, *As the Flower Withers* (1992); and another new member, Martin Powell, played violin and piano on the next album, *Turn Loose the Swans*, released in 1994.

The band produced another EP before their third album, *The Angel and the Dark River*, in 1995.

A style more akin to Pink Floyd was evident towards the end of the decade. Other notable albums have included *34.788% . . . Complete* (1998) and *The Light at the End of the World* (1999), *Meisterwerk I* (2000) and *II* (2001) and *The Dreadful Hours* (2001).

Napalm Death

As we saw in the chapter entitled 'Rock is a Hard Place', Napalm Death brought grindcore to the metal repertoires. They've been going since 1982, having been formed in Birmingham (UK) by Nik Bullen (vocals), Darren Fideski (guitar) and Nick Ratledge (drums), among others.

Their first album was *Scum*, which was released in 1986. Oddly, this piece had a different line-up on each side. They followed up *Scum* with *From Enslavement to Obliteration* in 1988, but not after they'd done some serious touring and released two *John Peel Sessions* recordings.

There were fifty-four tracks on the second album, but quite a lot, it has to be said, lasted no more than a few seconds, leading some journalists to brand the band a bit of a joke. Not too much of a joke for the BBC2 programme *Arena* to base a heavy-metal special on them, though. *Harmony Corruption*, recorded in Florida, appeared in 1990, and, after one of the bands members, Mick Harris, left, there was more touring, before a fourth album, *Utopia Banished*.

One of the band's remarkable achievements was to sell a charity record, 'Nazi Punks Fuck Off', which raised money for anti-Nazi groups and has sold more than ten thousand copies.

Other notable albums from Napalm Death have been *Diatribes* (1996), *Words from the Exit Wound* (1998) and *Enemy of the Music Business* (2000).

Necrophobic

You'd have thought that perhaps 'Necrophilic' would have been a more appropriate name for a death-metal outfit. This Swedish band were formed in the early nineties in Sweden, and their name, we think, comes from a Slayer track of that name.

Their first album, *The Nocturnal Silence*, was released in 1993, and a second one, *Darkside*, came out two years later – a more melodic offering, with less power.

Obituary

Slow, sluggish riffs and vomited, guttural vocals typify this Florida band, formed in the eighties, whose first album, *Slowly We Rot* came out in 1989.

The early 'vocals' could claim that label only in that the voice was in there somewhere, but these recordings just didn't bother with words or the more melodic capabilities of the larynx, opting instead for very guttural burps and roars from their singer, John Tardy.

The band's first name was Xecutioner, but someone else was claiming that so they decided on Obituary.

James Murphy, formerly of Death, and who would go on to perform with Testament, Disincarnate and Cancer, among others, joined the band in 1990, but didn't remain long.

After a three-year break, the band recorded their fifth album, *Back from the Dead*, in 1997.

OVERKILL

This New York band were formed in 1983, having named themselves after an old Motörhead song. Their first album, *Feel the Fire*, came out in 1985, with a second album, *Taking Over*, released two years later.

It's one of those bands that tend to change line-up like some people change clothes, although Bobby Ellsworth (vocals) has remained loyal.

Other notable albums have been *I Hear Black* (1993), *Killing Kind* (1996) and *Coverkill* (1999).

PANTERA

This lot started out as a glam line-up in 1981 and brought out their first album, *Metal Magic*, in 1983. They don't like to talk of their glam past, and by the time of *Power Metal* in 1988 they'd acquired beards and tattoos along with more credibility.

They're now seen as a very hard-hitting band, with a mixture of grind and thrash.

Their singer, Phil Anselmo, 'died' after overdosing on heroin, and was revived by medics.

Notable albums over the years have included *Cowboys from Hell* (1990), *Far Beyond Driven* (1994) and *Official Live: 101 Proof* (1997).

PESTILENCE

This Dutch death band were formed in the late 1980s, and brought out their debut album, *Malleus Maleficarum*, in 1988.

Their music was widely seen as being innovative, and band members leaned more towards progressive rock, seeing the metal scene as rather limiting.

After three further albums – *Consuming Impulse* (1989), *Testimony of the Ancients* (1991) and *Spheres* (1993), they split.

PRAYING MANTIS

Praying Mantis were formed in 1977 by two Spanish-Greek brothers, Tino and Chris Troy, together with Mick Ranson on drums and Bob Angelo on guitar, and soon came to the attention of the heavy-metal scene in the UK.

They received a lot of interest from the famous DJ Neal Kay, who played their material extensively, and eventually three demo tracks were published in 1979 as a 'maxi' single, 'The Soundhouse Tapes'. Another demo found its way onto the *Metal for Muthas* compilation, and Mantis were up there with the likes of Iron Maiden. That was not the end of their relationship with Maiden, however, because they made it into the support slot of the first Maiden UK tour. Soon they were recording their debut album, *Time Tells No Lies*, still regarded as one of the best among the NWOBHM phenomenon.

The song 'Johnny Cool' was included on the BBC compilation *Metal Explosion*, and Praying Mantis went on to play at the 1981 Reading Festival.

After a further Reading Festival appearance, there was a line-up change and a name change. Praying Mantis was no more. Instead, they became a band called Stratus, and issued a 1985 album, *Throwing Shapes*. However, Mantis re-formed in 1990 and released an album, *Live At Last*. During the 1990s, more albums were produced – including three in studio and one live – and the band gained a deal of credibility in the East, especially Japan.

The album many fans consider to be Mantis's true masterpiece is *Nowhere To Hide*, released in 2000.

PUNGENT STENCH

Now there's a pleasant name – as was the title of the demo, *Mucus Secretion* (it isn't known whether the drummer's name really was Alex Wank, and, anyway, it would probably be pronounced Vank, which rather robs it of a certain charm).

The band disbanded in the mid-nineties after leaving a few albums behind: *For God Your Soul . . . For Me Your Flesh* (1990, *Been Caught Buttering* (1992), *Club Mondo Bizarre for Members Only* (1994) and *Praise the Names of the Musical Assassins* (1998).

PYOGENESIS

Although they got together in 1992, this band's first album – *Sweet X-Rated Nothings* – was not released until 1995. They had, however, brought out an eponymous EP in 1992 as their debut recording, and it was regarded as a good exemplar of doomdeath.

This German band began moving into more

experimental styles, and soon found themselves described as alternative rock, with their use of electronics. They became a popular band on the festival circuit, although never really made it big.

Among their albums have been *Twinaleblood* (1995), and *Mono . . . Or Will It Ever Be the Way It Used To Be* (1998).

ROTTING CHRIST

This band toured with such big hitters as Deicide in the late nineties, keeping them in the spotlight of the heavy-metal world. They're a Greek black-metal outfit in whose work are to be found the satanic themes of such bands as Bathory, along with a nod to the gothic. They've even had the term 'dark metal' applied to them.

Two of them are brothers, Sakis and Themis Tolis (guitar/vocals and drums, respectively), and they've brought out several albums as a pair.

SABBAT

These were an outfit that could take on the big metal bands from the United States, such was their quality.

Martin Walkyier on vocals, Fraser Craske on bass,

Andy Sneap on guitar and Simon Negus on drums formed the band in the mid-eighties, and their debut album came in 1988 with *History of a Time to Come*, followed by *Dreamweavers* in 1989 and *Morning Has Broken* in 1991.

After the debut album, though, Sneap and Walkyier couldn't agree on the musical direction of the band, with Walkyier wanting to do more pagan stuff. So he left the band and formed Skyclad, a folk-thrash outfit. Sneap then took on Ritchie Desmond as vocalist and another guitarist, Simon Jones, joined the line-up – but at that point Craske left.

After further changes to the line-up, the band members went their separate ways.

Saint Vitus

This Los Angeles band were performing doom long before many of the bands who practise it today.

Dave Chandler on guitar, Armando Acosta on drums, Scott Reagers on vocals and Mark Adams on bass formed the band in the early 1980s, and were regular performers at festivals.

They've influenced a number of the doom bands of later years, and among their notable albums have been *St Vitus* (1984, the debut album), *Born Too Late* (1986), *Heavier Than Thou* (1991) and *Die Healing* (1995).

SATYRICON

This band were formed by Satyr on vocal and guitar and Frost on drums in 1992 (see the entry for Darkthrone for more on Satyr, who runs the label, Moonfog).

This band's first demo, *The Forest is My Throne*, was a pagan affair with anti-Christian sentiments, and future releases were to follow this template.

Their debut album was *Dark Medieval Times* in 1994, and on the band's second album, *Nemesis Divina* (1998), a particularly raw edge was made possible – perhaps inevitable – by the guest appearance of the Darkthrone guitarist Kvedulv, a.k.a. Nocturno Culto.

The point at which the band could be said to have 'arrived', though, was with their third effort, *Rebel Extravaganza*, which was released in 1999.

SAXON

Saxon are another northern England grouping, formed in the late seventies. Their line-up then comprised Peter 'Biff' Byford (vocals), Graham Oliver (guitar), Paul Quinn (guitar), Steve Dawson (bass) and Pete Gill (drums).

They played a lot of clubs and pubs in those days, and were known as Son of a Bitch.

Eventually, Saxon – now with their more familiar

name – were in at the start of the NWOBHM scene, along with the likes of Def Leppard, Diamond Head, Tygers of Pan Tang, Iron Maiden, Sweet Savage, Samson, Raven and Venom.

Their first album, *Saxon*, was released in 1979 – a solid rock affair. But *Wheels of Steel* in 1980 turned the tide for them, and earned them two UK Top Twenty hits 'Wheels of Steel' and '747 (Strangers in the Night)'.

That year they also released *Strong Arm of the Law*, another heavy-metal outing, and *Denim and Leather* followed in 1981. The band toured the USA and were well received, and also appeared at Castle Donington's Monsters of Rock festival.

More albums followed throughout the eighties, including *The Eagle Has Landed* (1982), *Power and the Glory* (1983), *Innocence Is No Excuse* (1985), *Rock the Nations* (1986) and *Destiny* (1988).

Power and the Glory confirmed them as a major rock band, while *Innocence* was more suited to radio audiences, but with *Rock the Nations* they were back to the old Saxon, unremittingly so.

Their nineties output has included *Roll Gypsies* (1990), *Solid Ball of Rock* (1991), *Dogs of War* (1995) and *Metalhead* (1999), with *Killing Ground* following in 2001.

Dogs of War brought with it some of the band's epic choruses of the eighties.

While Biff Byford and Paul Quinn carried on the official Saxon, Graham Oliver and Steve Dawson, who had left the band, with Pete Gill, who had left to join Motörhead as far back as 1984, were gigging together in the mid-nineties, and contesting the right to use the name Saxon. The issue was resolved eventually, with Oliver, Dawson and Gill winning the right to call themselves Oliver/Dawson Saxon.

SEPULTURA

These thrashers are a Brazilian outfit formed in 1984, releasing *Bestial Devastation*, a split EP, in 1985 with a band of fellow Brazilians called Overdose.

However, Sepultura didn't get much of a following until the release of their debut album, *Morbid Visions*, in 1986. *Arise* brought the band to international attention when it was released in 1991, but before that had come *Schizophrenia* (1987) and *Beneath the Remains* (1989).

By the time of their fifth album, *Chaos AD*, in 1993, the band had slowed a little. However, one fast track on this album was a highly political piece called 'Biotech Is Godzilla', written by Jello Biafra. It laid into and showed up the politicians who had ensured that the streets during the 1993 Rio Earth Summit had been free of vagrants, so that VIPs arriving for the proceedings would receive a healthier vision of the country to take back with them to their own. As so often, it takes art and music to show up just how low politicians can stoop.

More albums, followed, notable among them *Roots* in 1996 and *Against* in 1998.

SKYCLAD

Martin Walkyier, formerly of Sabbat, formed this band, the first to be called thrash-folk, along with Steve Ramsey, formerly of Pariah, Dave Pugh on guitar, Graeme English on bass, Fritha Jenkins on violin and Keith Baxter on drums.

'In general I haven't heard very much metal at all in the last few years that doesn't make me feel like I've heard it before.'

STEVE RAMSEY of Skyclad, interviewed on MetalUK.com

Their first album was *Wayward Sons of Mother Earth*, which was released in 1991, and this was followed in 1992 with *A Burnt Offering for the Bone Idol*. Folk metal had arrived, and Skyclad (the word, incidentally, is a Wiccan term for naked) have gained huge popularity, with other notable albums being *Irrational Anthems* and *Oui Avant-garde A Chance* in 1996 and *Vintage Whine* in 1999.

SLAYER

This LA outfit took thrash to a much wider public after it had featured on Metallica's first album, and made a big impression on the death-metal scene, too.

They got together in 1982, at first calling themselves Dragonslayer. Their stage shows included cover versions of pieces by Iron Maiden, Judas Priest and other similar bands. Their first album, *Show No Mercy* was released in 1983, with 'Metal Warfare' taking the dubious distinction of being the fastest song ever recorded (then, at least: it's been beaten since).

The speed continued with a pair of EPs, *Haunting the Chapel* and *Live Undead*, in 1984, and their next album, *Hell Awaits*, was issued in 1985.

The album *Reign in Blood* was released in 1986, but ran into controversy and CBS, as distributor, refused to handle it. This was because one of the songs, 'Angel of Death', concerned – and depicted in explicit detail – the dirty doings of the Nazi scientist Josef Mengele. However, it was distributed by Geffen eventually, and, as they say, all publicity is good publicity.

South of Heaven was the band's next album. This came out three years after *Reign in Blood*, and was followed two years later, in 1990, by *Seasons in the Abyss*.

Slayer did the legendary Clash of the Titans tour in the early 1990s along with other big names such as Anthrax and Megadeth.

Their next album, *Decade of Aggressions*, released in 1993, was a double live affair, and *Divine Intervention* followed in 1994. Other notables have been *Undisputed Attitude* in 1996 and the wonderfully titled *Diabolus In Musica* in 1998.

Slipknot

This outrageous and rather disgusting band call their fans 'maggots', and they wear overalls and masks on stage. Part of their act involves projectile-vomiting through the masks, and shitting on stage, throwing the turds into the crowd. But – they have one hell of a following.

'We put the masks on because we're musicians and we play music, man. We're kind of rebelling against [the continued commercialism of modern music; musicians doing Calvin Klein ads, etc.]. Obviously, our masks have a great look, but the reason that we started doing it in the first place was because we'd seen so many fucking bands suck the money dick and just completely cheese out to where they would get onstage and they'd be like "Hey, look! Do you like my new hairdo?" "Cool!" "D'ya like my new shirt that I bought on Santa Monica Boulevard today?" "Cool!" "Here's my new shoes, I'm endorsed." "Cool!" It's like "Fuck you, man! Play your fuckin' music!" Nobody gives a shit, they want to fuckin' hear your music.
And that's why we did the masks, that's why we did the coveralls, that's why we did all those things. We were like "Fuck my face! Here's my mask, this is what the music turns me into."'

COREY TAYLOR of Slipknot

Slipknot are of the brutal thrash world, and as we write this in mid-2002, they are on an eighteen-month world tour (more colourful facts about them are to be found on pages 56-9).

*'The other night on stage, I freaked out,
grabbed our drummer Chris,
threw him down and broke two
of his fucking fingers.
Why? You tell me. I was bored,
and that's the only god I've got.'*

**SHAWN CRAHAN of Slipknot,
Guardian, February 2002**

This Iowa-based band appeal mainly to teenagers, probably because of the bizarre nature of the stage act performed by their line-up of nine, and the fact that they always wear their costumes when appearing in public.

The man behind Slipknot is Shawn Crahan, known as Clown, who has turned his band into nothing less than a cult among teens. Clown takes on stage a jar containing a rotting crow's carcass, and a quick sniff has the desired effect on his stomach, allowing him to puke in CinemaScope and Technicolor, much to the delight of the young maggots.

The band produced a limited-edition album in 1996 called *Mate. Feed. Kill. Repeat*, which was a rebellion against the conservative nature of their state of Iowa. This was followed by an eponymous album, released twice under the same name but with a few differences.

TESTAMENT

Testament were once called Legacy, and began life sounding much like Metallica before ploughing their own furrow in the world of thrash metal. A Californian outfit, they've moved into death metal in the nineties, which has been put down to their recruiting the guitarist James Murphy.

At some point in their career, three drummers from Slayer have played with Testament, whose first album, *The Legacy*, was issued in 1987. Two more successful albums – *The New Order* and *Practice What You Preach* – followed in 1988 and 1989 respectively.

In 1994, the band got out of their contract with Atlantic, because they weren't happy with the company's promotion skills, after the release of *Low*, and subsequent albums have come to us through

Burnt Offerings, Mayhem and Spitfire.

Low was followed by *Live at the Fillmore* in 1996 and *Demonic* in 1997, while other notable albums have included another 1997 release, *Signs of Chaos* and *The Gathering* in 1999.

TYGERS OF PAN TANG

Another NWOBHM band, this one was born in Newcastle upon Tyne in 1978 and comprised Jess Cox (vocals), Rob Weir (guitar), Richard 'Rocky' Laws (bass) and Brian 'Big' Dick (drums).

Newcastle's Neat label released their debut EP. It was the label's first rock release, and it soon topped the metal charts.

After they'd signed to MCA and done an album in 1980, *Wild Cat*, there were some line-up changes, when Cox left and in came Jon Deverill and John Sykes.

After the band's third album, *Crazy Nights*, John Sykes left and was replaced by Fred Purser, formerly of a band called Penetration.

The Cage was released in 1982, and this established the band in the States, but after disputes with MCA their career came to an end, with Cox forming Tyger Tyger in 1986.

Unleashed

Johnny (vocals and bass guitar), Tomas (guitar), Fredrik (guitar) and Anders on drums formed this Swedish band in the early nineties, concentrating on solid metal and a macho image.

Taking their cue from Manowar and Iron Maiden, they attracted a reasonable fan base in Europe, and brought out four albums, *Where No Life Dwells* in 1991, *Shadows in the Deep* a year later, *Across the Open Sea* in 1993 and, in 1994, *Live in Vienna*.

These were followed by *Victory* in 1995, *Eastern Blood* in 1996 and *Warrior* in 1997.

Obviously wishing to be fair to their fans – but not wanting to miss out on a few krona, either – the band responded to an overpriced bootleg of one of their live shows, and brought out their 1994 album, *Live in Vienna*, to queer its pitch.

Venom

Extreme metal started here, with Venom – or so many of Venom's fans would tell you. They would also tell you that Metallica's *Kill 'Em All* owed much to Venom.

They started life in Newcastle in the late seventies, but were then called Oberon, and comprised Conrad Lant (a.k.a. Cronos) on bass and vocals, Jeff Dunn (Mantas) on guitar and Tony Bray (Abaddon) on drums.

Their first album, *Welcome to Hell* (1981), established their fast bluesy style and the second and third, *Black Metal* (1982) and *At War with Satan* (1984) brought a new approach to the metal genre, containing, as they did, influences of Black Sabbath and Judas Priest.

But then big US bands such as Anthrax and Metallica took up the Venom sound and made it something of their own, although Venom did hang on to their loyal fan base in the UK and continental Europe.

After *At War with Satan* came *Possessed* in 1985, and *Eine Kleine Nachtmusic* followed in 1986, after which Dunn left the band, and was replaced by two guitarists, Mike Hickey and Jimmy Clare, who performed on the 1987 album, *Calm Before the Storm*.

Albums in the nineties have included *Temples of Ice* in 1991, *Black Reign* in 1996 and *Cast in Stone* in 1997. Their 2000 album *Resurrection* received enormous acclaim.

WARFARE

This UK band combined punk and thrash and were clearly influenced by the likes of Motörhead and Venom.

They were formed in the early eighties by their

drummer and singer Evo, and their debut in 1984 was *Pure Filth*, which was followed the following year by *Metal Anarchy*.

Conrad Lant (a.k.a. Cronos, of Venom) produced their third album, *Mayhem, Fuckin' Mayhem*, in 1986, and fans had to wait two years for *Conflict of Hatred* and a further two years before *Hammer Horror*.

After *Mayhem . . .*, though, the band failed to keep up to fans' expectations, and they disbanded after their last album, *A Crescendo of Reflections*, which was issued in 1991.

XENTRIX

Sounding much like Metallica, Xentrix formed in 1987, although they were called Sweet Vengeance then. Another bunch of British northern lads – this time from Preston in Lancashire – they recorded a demo, *Hunger for . . .*, and were signed up to Roadrunner, who released their first album, *Shattered Existence*, in 1989.

Xentrix have another claim to fame (or infamy, depending on which side of the legal divide you were on), in that they released a twelve-inch single of the theme to the film *Ghostbusters*, and Columbia Pictures were miffed because the band had used the *Ghostbusters* logo.

Xentrix went on to release another album in 1990,

For Whose Advantage?, showing them to be doing more than regurgitating the style of Metallica.

The band parted company in 1992, having released *Dilute to Taste* in 1991 and *Kin* in 1992, but got back together with a new singer and recorded their fifth album, *Scourge*, but they split up once again.

The Wizardry of Ozz:
OZZY OSBOURNE,
THE FATHER OF METAL

*'I don't want it to end. I mean, what the fuck
does a lunatic do when he retires?'*

OZZY OSBOURNE

In the beginning was the word, and the word was Ozzy – although he was known then as John Michael Osbourne, born in Aston, Birmingham, UK, on 3 December 1948, to John and Lillian. He was one of four children then, but would soon be one of six.

He was not a good boy right from the start, and was forever getting into trouble at school for ditching his uniform, sneaking off to coffee bars, illicitly smoking with his pals. Ozzy was a typical backstreet boy. He also had a thing about gore and the darker side of life – an obsession that was to characterize his music-making from then till now.

He formed his first band, the Black Panthers, when he was just fourteen, but suffered for his musical tastes at that time, and was once caught by his pals singing 'I Want To Hold Your Hand', the Beatles hit. He was punched and kicked for it.

Ozzy had a series of jobs on leaving school – labouring, as assistant to a local plumber, factory work, apprentice toolmaker. But his real lure was the local slaughterhouse where, he said in an interview, he 'loved killing animals'. The notorious incident with the bat – he bit off its head on stage in Iowa in 1982 – although in fact an accident (he mistook the live creature for a rubber one of the kind fans often threw onstage), can be set into context when you realize that Osbourne had said in that interview that killing animals 'was definitely my forte. I used to stick them, stab them, chop them, totally torture the fuckers to death. And if the pigs had worms I used to bite their heads off. Even back then the people I worked with thought I was mad, too outrageous.'

*'Bad language isn't second nature
to me: it's first. Bad language
and bad behaviour.'*

OZZY OSBOURNE

He told Rolling Stone Online in May 1997, 'It took a lot of water to down just that fucking bat's head, let me tell you. It's still stuck in my fucking throat, after all these years. People all over the world say, "You're the guy who kills creatures? You still do it? You do it every night?" It happened fucking once, for Christ's sake.'

Hard to think this heavily tattooed man who popped drugs as if there were no tomorrow was one of the line-up for the Queen's Golden Jubilee celebrations in summer 2002, along with establishment figures such as *Sir* Paul McCartney and *Sir* Elton John, and the cute *Pop Idol* winner Will Young.

> *'I've got so many tattoos*
> *that I look like a road map.'*
>
> **OZZY OSBOURNE**

This short book is not the place for a full biography – for that we can recommend *Ozzy Unauthorized* by Sue Crawford (London, Michael O'Mara Books, 2002) – but what follow are some of the highlights of this weird man's remarkable career, which continued ignominiously, for in 1965 Ozzy served six weeks in

Winson Green Prison, Birmingham, for burglary.

Between 1965 and 1967 he sang briefly with three bands, Music Machine, Approach and Rare Breed, and joined Tony Iommi, Terry ('Geezer') Butler and Bill Ward to form the Polka Tulk Blues Band in 1968. This would soon get a new name, Earth, and would tour both in Britain and continental Europe.

The band that is arguably the one that 'invented' heavy metal (although no one can claim to have invented something that evolves: there is just a seminal moment when you realize it's there) came into being in 1969, when Earth changed its name to Black Sabbath. This coincided with the heavier musical style that would be associated with the band and its imitators. With it came the band's association with darkness – or perhaps that should be Darkness, with a capital 'D', for Satanism and the occult.

'Evil Woman' was the band's first demo single, and was released in Britain in 1970. That was January. By 13 February, the band's eponymous first album was recorded in just twelve hours and released on the Vertigo label. *Black Sabbath* was then released in the USA by Warner Brothers, and the band toured American colleges.

A second album was not far away: they released *Paranoid* in September that year, and *Master of Reality* came out in July 1971. The band did another tour of the States that year.

Ozzy Osbourne married Thelma Mayfair (who already had a son, Elliot) in 1971. In 1972 the band released *Volume 4*, and that same year Osbourne and Thelma had their first child, Jessica.

'When we did that album [Volume 4]
it was like one big Roman orgy – we'd
be in the Jacuzzi all day doing coke,
and every now and then we'd
get up to do a song.'

OZZY OSBOURNE

Another album, *Sabbath, Bloody Sabbath*, was released in Britain in 1973, and in April 1974 Black Sabbath were at the California Jam in Ontario, California. That same year, Ozzy met Sharon Arden (whom he was to marry in July 1982, after the break-up of his marriage to Thelma).

In 1975, Ozzy and Thelma's son Louis was born. *Sabotage* was released in the UK that same year, as was a compilation double disc, *We Sold Our Soul for Rock 'n' Roll*. The following year the band sacked their managers, Patrick Meehan and Wilf Pine, whom they'd taken on in 1970 after sacking Jim Simpson as manager. The new man was Don Arden, Sharon's father.

Technical Ecstasy was released in Britain in 1976 and in November 1977 Osbourne left the band – but returned two months later.

Jack Osbourne, Ozzy's father, died in January 1978, and later that year *Never Say Die* was released. That was also a turning point for Osbourne: he toured with Sabbath for the last time, and was sacked at the end of the tour in December.

It was time for a solo career, and he signed with Don Arden's Jet Records, releasing his first solo album, *Blizzard of Ozz,* the following year in September, when he also began a tour of Britain, beginning in Glasgow. It wasn't just bats' heads Osbourne took a liking to: he bit the head off a live dove during a meeting with Epic Records in LA in 1981, and he and Sharon were kicked out. But the publicity was good for his tour, and be began another – this time of the USA – in May 1981 to support *Blizzard of Ozz*. That same year Thelma and Ozzy's marriage broke up and they were divorced.

Ozzy released his second solo album, *Diary of a Madman*, on 31 October 1981 (meanwhile, Black Sabbath released *Mob Rules*). The following January, Osbourne performed the infamous bat routine in front of an audience at Des Moines, Iowa, and as a result was banned in Boston.

In February 1982, in San Antonio, Texas, Ozzy was drunk and decided to take a leak on the Alamo. Big mistake. The arresting officer told him, 'Son, when you piss on the Alamo you piss on the state of Texas.' Ozzy – who was wearing a green evening dress of his wife's at the time – is reported as saying to police who were about to arrest him, 'But it was a genuine mistake and, anyway, when the Mexicans were attacking it there must have been more than just piss running down the walls!' As a result of being 'caught short', as he put it, Ozzy was banned from playing again in San Antonio (a ban that was lifted, however, in 1992).

(Some years later, Ozzy is reported as saying, 'If you go out for a drink, you go out for a drink. You don't think, "I'll have a few pints; I'll piss up this shrine. I'm going to punch this copper in the nose; then I'm going home, strangle my wife and fucking throw the dog on the fire." That's not your plan, but you end up doing stupid shit like that. I kind of accept it but I'm not really proud of it. It's not something I'll say to my grandchildren: "You know what I did when I was your age?"')

Tragedy struck the following month to the day: 19 March 1982. In Florida, Ozzy's guitarist and co-star Randy Rhoads was killed in a plane crash (a tribute album, *Tribute*, was released five years later, March 1987).

Sharon Arden and Ozzy Osbourne were married in

Maui, Hawaii, on Independence Day 1982, and that same year, in order to fulfil a contract with Don Arden, he released *Talk of the Devil*, a double album of Sabbath songs.

A lot happened for Osbourne in 1983: in May he played at the USA Festival in San Bernardino, California, for a third of a million spectators, and in September Aimee was born. Now managed by his wife Sharon, Ozzy released *Bark at the Moon* in 1983. The following October saw another birth, that of Kelly, but on the very next day Ozzy booked a stay at the Betty Ford Clinic.

In 1985 he played a Live Aid concert in Philadelphia, having teamed up with the original Sabbath members Tony Iommi, Geezer Butler and Bill Ward. Another birth happened in November that year, when Jack entered the world, a year and a month after Kelly.

Back in October 1984, a young man called John McCollum had shot himself in the head while listening to 'Suicide Solution', one of the tracks from Osbourne's 1980 album *Blizzard of Ozz*, and in January 1986 the youth's parents sued Osbourne and CBS Records, saying that listening to the song had caused his suicide.

The song had been written after the former AC/DC singer Bon Scott had died after a booze binge. Part of the lyric goes:

Wine is fine
But whiskey's quicker.
Suicide is slow with liquor.
Take a bottle, drain your sorrows;
Then it floods away tomorrows.

It was a case that would drag on, and it wasn't until October 1992 that the Supreme Court upheld an earlier ruling that Osbourne was protected by the First Amendment – the one that deals with free speech: 'Congress shall make no law respecting an establishment of religion, or prohibiting the free exercise thereof; or abridging the freedom of speech, or of the press; or the right of the people peaceably to assemble, and to petition the government for a redress of grievances.'

'Parents have called me and said,
"When my son died of a drug overdose your
record was on the turntable." I can't help that.
These people are freaking out anyway
and they need a vehicle
for their freak-outs.'

OZZY OSBOURNE

However, the thought that one of his fans had killed himself as a result of listening to one of Osbourne's lyrics was an upsetting experience for him.

But back to the 1980s, and in the early summer of 1987 Osbourne took the role of the Rev. Aaron Gilstrom in a horror movie, *Trick or Treat*, and not long after he began a tour of British prisons.

He released *No Rest for the Wicked* in October 1988, and he began another US tour about then.

In August 1989, Ozzy teamed up with Bon Jovi, Mötley Crüe, Skid Row and The Scorpions to play at the Moscow Music Peace Festival. The following month, he attacked his wife, Sharon, and was jailed, but was released with a condition that he go into rehab for three months, which he did, and they got back together once he was released in December.

'If I was to add ecstasy to my prescription drugs, I'd explode. There'd be a pair of shoes on the floor and a splat on the ceiling!'

OZZY OSBOURNE

Geezer Butler and Ozzy got together in 1990 to release a live EP, *Just Say Ozzy*, and in August that year a compilation album of old material was released by Priority Records: *Ten Commandments*.

More lawsuits were in store for Osbourne after two teenagers shot themselves in Georgia in the USA, and their parents blamed his music for their deaths. As we've seen, the Supreme Court was to confirm in 1992 that he was protected by the First Amendment. A District Court judge had dismissed the lawsuits, anyway, again citing the First Amendment, in May 1991.

In September that year both *No More Tears* and the video *Don't Blame Me: The Tales of Ozzy Osbourne* were released, and the following month Osbourne played at the Foundations Forum convention in LA.

Ozzy had to cancel part of his US tour in November 1991 after he had broken his foot on stage in Chicago in October, and the foot had become infected. But he resumed in Florida in January 1992. In March that year, a memorial concert for Randy Rhoads was held in California, and two days later, after he'd invited audience members on to the stage at a concert at Laguna Hills in California, $100,000 in damage was caused and Ozzy was slightly hurt.

Ozzy began a tour called No More Tours in June that year, and was to release a double album, *Live and Loud*, a year later recorded at some of its concerts.

November 1992 saw a Black Sabbath reunion, when a concert was held at the Pacific Amphitheater in Costa Mesa, California, and Ozzy was joined for a half-hour set by Geezer Butler, Tony Iommi and Bill Ward. Three days later, Black Sabbath got a star on the Rock Walk on Sunset Boulevard in Hollywood.

The much-coveted Grammy Award came Ozzy's way in 1993, when he received the Best Metal Performance honour for 'I Don't Want to Change the World'. And an accolade of another kind awaited him in 1994, when he got to star with one of the most famous female entertainers of all time: Miss Piggy. He did a duet with her on *The Muppet Show*, singing 'Born to Be Wild', and it was released on a children's album called *Kermit Unpigged*.

Nativity in Black – A Tribute to Black Sabbath came out in 1994, with Ozzy joining Therapy? to sing 'Iron Man'.

The following year Ozzy flew to Paris to record *Ozzmosis* and in August that year he set off on a series of American and European tours, beginning in Monterey, Mexico. He was back in the States – Denver in Colorado – in December that year to launch his Retirement Sucks tour, ending with five concerts in Japan the following March.

It was in 1996 that a series of concerts called Ozzfest began, this one in September with two expanded Ozzfest concerts in Phoenix, Arizona, and

San Bernardino in California in October. As you would expect, from these came a video and album, predictably called *Ozzfest Live!*, and featuring not just Osbourne but other bands from the concerts.

Ozzfest '97 began in May, and Ozzy began playing with his own band and with Tony Iommi, Geezer Butler, and in November he released *The Ozzman Cometh*, a greatest-hits album. Black Sabbath got back together in December of that year for two shows at Birmingham's National Exhibition Centre.

A European tour followed in May 1998, as Osbourne toured with his band. The tour included performances by Black Sabbath. There were two Ozzfests in 1998, the first at Milton Keynes in June and US Ozzfest '98 began at Holmdel in New Jersey.

'I have a message for anyone coming to the Ozzfest this summer [2000]: if you're planning to jump up onstage during my set, please do not give me any bear hugs, because they fucking hurt.'

OZZY OSBOURNE

Black Sabbath's *Reunion*, a double CD with Osbourne on vocals, recorded in Birmingham the previous year, was released, and went platinum in February 1999. Three months later, in May, the fourth Ozzfest began, featuring Black Sabbath. This was claimed to be the last time Sabbath would tour, and so it was dubbed the Last Supper Tour. Black Sabbath played two shows in Birmingham in December 1999 and said these would be their last together, but Ozzy played a show in Los Angeles for KROQ radio and surprised everyone by reuniting with the band.

'I'm still as crazy as ever. I still go on the stage and do my best to be a bit more crazy every day. I guarantee if people come and see this show they'll be talking about it for years. I live out a lot of people's fantasies. It's so amazing.'

OZZY OSBOURNE

By 2001, Ozzy Osbourne was into his fifties – just – and the strains of touring had begun to be felt. Ozzy was ill, and began to consult a number of doctors. A nodule appeared in his throat and a number of concerts had to be postponed. (These days, he walks with a slight limp and has poor hearing. His hands shake at times and there have been rumours that he has suffered a stroke or has Parkinson's disease, although he denies that.)

'I'm glued together with medication. If I don't pop pills I lose it. I'm a fucking nutter.'

OZZY OSBOURNE

Ozzy's mother, Lillian, died in April 2001, from complications brought on by her diabetes, which gutted Ozzy. He did play his Ozzfest '01 concert at Milton Keynes, though, along with Black Sabbath, and his first solo album for six years, *Down To Earth,* was released in October that year.

In November ten dates had to be postponed after he slipped in the shower before a concert in Arizona, and suffered a stress fracture in a leg. By December, however, he was playing an emotional benefit show in New Jersey for victims of the World Trade Center atrocity.

MTV viewers in both the UK and USA will be familiar with the fly-on-the-wall documentary series *The Osbournes*, which began showing in March 2002 in the States and May in the UK. It was a smash hit.

A great moment for the ailing Ozzy came in April 2002, when he was induced into the Rock and Roll Hall of Fame, and in May that year he and Sharon had dinner with President Bush at the White House. It is said that Ozzy greeted the President by pointing to his long, stringy, pink and brown hair and saying 'You should wear your hair like mine!' Bush quipped, 'Second term, Ozzy!'

The man who bit a bat's head off, who has experimented with every drug going and who seems to find any sentence semantically challenged if it doesn't contain at least one F-word, entertained the British Queen in June 2002 when she celebrated her Golden Jubilee with (among other things) a concert at Buckingham Palace.

It is ironic that rebellion and the old fuddy-duddy Establishment should embrace each other eventually.

*'As long as there are kids who are
pissed off and have no real way
[of] venting out that anger,
heavy metal will live on.'*

OZZY OSBOURNE

Bibliography

This isn't a definitive bibliography, but will give the reader interested in knowing more about the world of heavy metal a few titles to browse in the bookshops or at an online bookseller such as Amazon. Browsing leads to more links and recommendations and you'll soon have a library devoted to this distinctive brand of popular music.

Aerosmith and Stephen Davis,
Walk This Way: The Autobiography of Aerosmith
(Virgin Books) ('Walk This Way' is an Aerosmith
song from the album *Toys in the Attic*)

Almond, Steve,
My Life in Heavy Metal
(Heinemann)

Arnett, Jeffrey Jensen,
*Metalheads: Heavy Metal Music and Adolescent
Alienation* (Westview Press)

Crawford, Sue,
Ozzy Unauthorized
(Michael O'Mara Books)

Hale, Mark,
*Headbangers: The Worldwide Mega-Book of
Heavy Metal Bands*
(Popular Culture)

Kendall, Paul, and Dave Lewis (compilers),
Led Zeppelin: In Their Own Words
(Omnibus Press)

McIver, Joel,
Extreme Metal
(Omnibus Press)

Moynihan, Michael, and Dirk Soderlind,
*Lords of Chaos: The Bloody Rise of the Satanic Metal
Underground*
(Feral House)

Popoff, Martin,
Goldmine Heavy Metal Record Price Guide
(Krause Publications)

Putterford, Mark,
Metallica: In Their Own Words
(Omnibus Press)

Sharpe-Young, Gary,
The Rockdetector A–Z of Black Metal
(Cherry Red Books)

Shaw, Harry,
Ozzy Osbourne: In His Own Words
(Omnibus Press)

Strong, Martin C,
The Great Metal Discography
(Canongate Books)

Weiner, Chuck,
Marilyn Manson
(Omnibus Press)

Weinstein, Deena,
Heavy Metal: The Music and Its Culture
(Da Capo Press)